On Becoming a School Principal

*From a Humble Beginning as a Country Schoolteacher
to Leadership of an Innovative Elementary School*

G. Wayne Mosher

> August 15 2021
> For Marcia Kampelman
> A warm hearted person who gets it about ding for others, and that care about what she is doing to sweeten my world.
> Richard Oxenfart

ARCHWAY PUBLISHING

Copyright © 2021 G. Wayne Mosher.

All rights reserved. No part of this book may be used or reproduced by any means, graphic, electronic, or mechanical, including photocopying, recording, taping or by any information storage retrieval system without the written permission of the author except in the case of brief quotations embodied in critical articles and reviews.

This book is a work of non-fiction. Unless otherwise noted, the author and the publisher make no explicit guarantees as to the accuracy of the information contained in this book and in some cases, names of people and places have been altered to protect their privacy.

Archway Publishing books may be ordered through booksellers or by contacting:

Archway Publishing
1663 Liberty Drive
Bloomington, IN 47403
www.archwaypublishing.com
844-669-3957

Because of the dynamic nature of the Internet, any web addresses or links contained in this book may have changed since publication and may no longer be valid. The views expressed in this work are solely those of the author and do not necessarily reflect the views of the publisher, and the publisher hereby disclaims any responsibility for them.

Any people depicted in stock imagery provided by Getty Images are models, and such images are being used for illustrative purposes only. Certain stock imagery © Getty Images.

ISBN: 978-1-6657-0652-0 (sc)
ISBN: 978-1-6657-0653-7 (hc)
ISBN: 978-1-6657-0651-3 (e)

Library of Congress Control Number: 2021908463

Print information available on the last page.

Archway Publishing rev. date: 05/27/2021

To Dr. Richard Overfelt, teachers, and staff who opened Highcroft Ridge Elementary School in 1978

CONTENTS

Acknowledgments xi
Prologue xiii

Chapter 1 Origins of a School Leader 1
           Growing up in the Great Depression 1
           The Return to Duncans Bridge 3

Chapter 2 The Life of a Country Schoolteacher 5
           Life in a Small Town 5
           Escaping the Depression 6
           Finding a Sense of Direction 8
           Teaching in a One-Room Country School 11
           Last in the Box 13
           Developing Credibility 14
           Becoming Aware of Personal and
           Professional Worth 16
           Summary 17

Chapter 3 Research Methods 20
           Ethnography 20
           Origins of the Study 21
           Sources of Data 22
           The Organizational Plan of the Book 23

Chapter 4 Planning a New School 24
           The Architecture of an Open-Plan School 24
           Educational Change: A Familiar but Complex
           Process 27

	Temporary Systems: A Training Model 29
	The First Staff Meeting 31
	Beliefs as an Expression of Formal Doctrine 32
	Steps in Building a Staff 35
	The Good Person Ethic 36
	Getting Organized 40
	Summary 41
Chapter 5	The Long March to the Opening of School 44
	Important Topics on the February Agenda 44
	Task Force Groups—Parent Volunteers 47
Chapter 6	Building a School Community 50
	Origin of Richard's Ideas about Community 50
	Dialogue with Parents 53
Chapter 7	Substantive Additions to the Planning Schedule 57
	Looking Ahead 57
	Important Elements in the Final Months of Planning 58
	The Prominence of the Reading Curriculum 60
Chapter 8	Highcroft Ridge Elementary School Takes Flight 70
	Orientation 70
	Public Relations 74
	Addressing Last-Minute Issues 76
Chapter 9	The First Day of School 79
	Organized and Prepared 79
	Lunch Procedures 80
	A Successful First Day 81
Chapter 10	Teaching in an Open-Plan School 83
	First Encounters with Flexible Space 83
	September 14: Open House 87
	Ongoing Adjustments to Lunch Procedure 89
	September 29: Richard Overfelt Recognition Day 94
	Formal Patterns of Staff and Pupil Recognition 98
	The Parent Volunteer Program Is Launched 100

Chapter 11	The Pursuit of Collaboration	102
	Assumptions about Team Teaching	102
	Statewide Testing	105
	Reading Program Adjustments	106
	Gradual Steps toward Collaboration	108
	Increasing Stress	112
	Summary	116
Chapter 12	Analysis and Implications	121
	Introduction	121
	Nature or Nurture	122
	Awakened Leadership	123
	Expansion of the Principal's Responsibilities	124
	The Collaborative School	126
	Pitfalls in Selection of the Right People	128
	Professional Development of Teachers	131
	Educational Change	133
	Educational Change: An Imperfect Process	134
	Implications for the Future	136

Epilogue		139
	Introduction	139
	Initial Impressions	139
	Staff Meeting	141
	Creative Teaching, Staffing, and Collaborative Planning in Open Space	142
	Enter the New Superintendent	144
	Sustainability	153
	Professional Development and Teaching the "Good Person Ethic"	155
	Final Thoughts	160
References		165

ACKNOWLEDGMENTS

I want to extend my appreciation to Dr. Richard Overfelt, teachers, and staff who allowed me to be part of the planning and implementation of Highcroft Ridge Elementary School in 1978. They included me in a special moment in their professional lives by providing access to their classes, team meetings, and school events. The year that I spent with them was more than instructive; it opened my eyes to the complexities of teaching children and building a community of learners. I will always be grateful.

The project took years to complete, and I couldn't have finished without the interest and support of my family. Words cannot express my appreciation for their patience and understanding. Given that I grew up in the typewriter age, I needed a good deal of help using the computer. Thanks to my daughter Megan who provided assistance with technology, and to Spencer Wheelehan, who developed graphics for the manuscript. Special thanks to Jane Greer, a former English teacher, who shared expert proofing and editing, and to Dr. Mary Ellen Finch for her review of the manuscript and encouragement. Thanks also to Denise Francisco, who gave important assistance with the manuscript in the early stages of writing. Finally, although he is no longer with us, I would be remiss if I didn't acknowledge Dr. Louis Smith, who patiently introduced me to qualitative methods of research.

I have had several great teachers in the past, and Richard Overfelt was one of the best. He has been a friend and supportive influence in shaping my career as a high school principal.

PROLOGUE

There was a time in American history when children were educated in one-room country schools, governed by local boards of education with shoestring budgets, few amenities, and teachers who lacked formal training. Within these schools, children received a foundation for life in a democratic society. Country schools dominated the largely rural landscape for more than a hundred years, eventually fading away with urbanization and school consolidation. Teaching during that era relied on rudimentary textbooks, simple lessons, recitation, and hands-on learning activities. Children were expected to volunteer for tasks such as retrieving water from the well, collecting firewood for the stove, cleaning blackboards, and the most valued task of all: raising and lowering the flag each day.

Country schools were important institutions valued by the communities they served. In contrast, support for present-day schools seems to fluctuate in a sea of concerns expressed in the public dialogue. Noted education historian Diane Ravitch (2001) defined the current struggle as "The Troubled Crusade," dominated by a complexity of factors such as education funding, legislative mandates, increasing diversity, education of handicapped children, racial issues, school violence, poverty, and the failure of school reform efforts, among others as sources of disaffection.

In recent history, public education has become highly politicized. Reforms have largely centered on student achievement and formalized testing procedures as measures of progress. From nominal beginnings, the testing movement has resulted in significant expenditures for test development, with little to no evidence of improved achievement. With each new administration, the nation has taken on a new mantra. In the 1990s, reform was formalized in the No Child Left Behind Act. In the early 2000s, it was called Race to the Top, while in the current administration, reform shifted to charter and private school education at the expense of public schools. None of these politically driven reforms have significantly improved achievement, but state and national education agencies continue to pursue testing programs as the focal point for school reform.

In his book *Schools for Tomorrow* written in 1915, John Dewey argued for a genre of research that focused on school-based inquiry as a means for promoting the improvement of schools. His point of view was lost in the reductionist view of education research prominent at that time. This view assumed that the collective knowledge from research would produce a holistic understanding of schooling. My argument is not with the role of scientific inquiry but the utilization of a wider range of methods such as case studies, participant observation, and ethnography as a means of understanding complex systems like schools. Adherents to school-based research studies, some of which are cited in this book, may be more useful to education reformers.

This book is written in the spirit of John Dewey and his advocacy for school-based research initiatives designed and implemented by practitioners. It is intended for an audience of educators and parents who want to help schools be the best that they can be. The narrative examines how one man rose from humble beginnings to leadership of a new, innovative school. It is an ethnography of a school principal and a group of teachers in the act of doing good things for children.

CHAPTER 1
Origins of a School Leader

Growing up in the Great Depression

The stock market crash in October 1929 heralded the start of the Great Depression, which plunged the country into one of the darkest periods in American history. Money was in short supply, unemployment was rampant, and vast numbers of people relied on soup kitchens and charity for survival. People in rural areas were particularly hard hit when bank closures prevented farmers from securing loans they depended on for planting the next year's crops.

Ten years earlier, following World War I, another economic crisis occurred that was every bit as serious. Farmers were crawling out from under one crisis to face yet another one that was far more ominous. Richard Overfelt was born into this world on July 18, 1929. The little town of Duncans Bridge, nestled in the Northeast Missouri farm country, was home during his early years.

The Overfelts lived in a white two-story home with a large wraparound front porch, built in the Southern style. It was perhaps the finest home in town, and it remains so in the present day. It was but a short distance from the Salt River forming the town's southern border. The home was a simple but elegant structure built by Richard's grandfather, Thomas Edward Overfelt, in the 1880s. Richard's parents, Thelma and Chester Overfelt, eventually occupied the home, which also served as a boardinghouse managed by his mother. Boarders included rural schoolteachers and a few students from other parts of the county who attended the local high school. Upon occasion, the Overfelt boardinghouse also accommodated men who worked on the roads.

As an only child, Richard received lots of attention from parents, boarders, and teachers. Some might say that all the adulation may have caused a bit of spoiling. Much of Richard's early life was immersed in Duncans Bridge and the adversity of the Depression, an era that influenced the direction of his life and future prospects.

In the late nineteenth century, Duncans Bridge was little more than a cluster of nondescript homes, a barbershop, general store, gas station, Methodist church, and a gristmill that depended on the energy of the Salt River to process grain from local farmers. There were no more than two dozen residents at that time. The collection of buildings was arranged along both sides of Highway 151, at that time a primitive dirt road. However, a county newspaper article described Duncans Bridge as a place with "significant economic potential," a prediction that would never materialize.

The region was dotted with many little communities like Duncans Bridge, dispersed through farmland that was originally prairie. In the early 1800s, pioneers from Virginia, Tennessee, and Kentucky settled there and began farming and raising cattle on the tall bluestem prairie grass. Rich soil, verdant pasture, and a moderate climate favored agriculture, which remains the primary industry today. The region was also known for Missouri mules, important in agriculture throughout Missouri. The nearby town of Clarence served as a railroad collection point for the export of mules throughout the United States and abroad for military service during the First World War.

The Return to Duncans Bridge

Richard and I returned to Duncans Bridge in the fall of 1999 to visit the town and the nearby Woodlawn School, where he began his teaching career in 1946. Although once a bustling place, the town had changed a great deal since the 1930s, when Richard was a boy. The businesses he remembered from that period had long since disappeared, and only a handful of dwellings; the school he attended, his former home, and old Duncans Bridge Methodist Church remained. Upon entering the church, I noticed a sign documenting the previous Sunday attendance: six people! The dilapidated remnants of Farmers Bank, founded by Richard's grandfather in the 1920s, was still visible, but like many rural banks, it closed during the Depression.

The Salt River still ambled through the south end of town, but aside from the church, there was little observable human activity. Over time, the population shifted to larger cities with better employment opportunities. Duncans Bridge was like an eddy turning slowly along the edge of a swirling river. In years past, little towns like Duncans Bridge were centers of community life where everyone knew and took care of each other. Richard often spoke fondly of the benevolence of people in Duncans Bridge, remembering how they responded to people in need. If you arrived at someone's home at mealtime, there would be a place for you at the table. People were enterprising and resilient in the face of adversity.

Most of us find it hard to conceive of life without electricity, but most rural communities had none until after the Depression. However, some of the folks in Duncans Bridge took matters in their own hands and created a limited electric grid of their own. They used a kerosene-powered generator to produce current through wiring they installed, and for the first time, homes had electricity. Independent and gritty, rural folks found a way to get things done.

Woodlawn School is located on a dirt road a few miles from Duncans Bridge, in the Woodlawn Township. The white clapboard building stood on an acre of ground, with tall trees surrounding the old playground, outhouses, and well. After the school was closed, it became a residence for a time and eventually shuttered permanently. However, the memories remained.

Richard and I wandered the school grounds talking about what it was like to teach in a one-room school with multiple grade levels and how he enjoyed playing games with children at recess. At seventeen, just graduated from high school, he was not much older than his students were, and he lacked experience in teaching. It was truly a virginal experience. No matter how tenuous the beginning, his experience at Woodlawn was the platform for a career covering more than seventy years and continues as this tome is written. It all began in the town of Duncans Bridge and Woodlawn School, in the vast rural setting of Northeast Missouri.

CHAPTER 2
The Life of a Country Schoolteacher

Life in a Small Town

As an only child, Richard lived among a large extended family of grandparents, aunts, uncles, and several cousins. Most were farmers who lived in and around Duncans Bridge. Richard described his parents as hardworking, caring people who provided guidance and affirmation but didn't closely monitor his activities. They held high expectations for appropriate behavior; this allowed Richard to make a few of his own decisions. Children were encouraged to be self-reliant and responsible in the pursuit of having fun. It was a time when parents commonly talked to other parents about inappropriate behavior among their children, especially in small communities, calling to mind the old African proverb "It takes a village to raise a child."

In addition to managing a boardinghouse, Richard's mother worked at the local general store that his parents eventually bought and operated. His father was a farmer, and in the 1930s, he was elected as a representative to the Agricultural Adjustment Administration, a government agency that advised farmers on ways to improve farm income. According to Richard, his father earned five dollars a day, which was considered very good pay during the Depression. In addition, he and two of his horses also maintained the local roads, which were always in need of repair. The elder Overfelt received a dollar a day for his labor—and a dollar each for the horses. Through these various endeavors, Richard's parents were able to have a secure but not privileged life during the Depression.

Escaping the Depression

Social events often included the extended Overfelt family gatherings, which didn't require extensive transportation. Travel was expensive, and the Overfelts' car often sat idle for lack of funds for license and fuel. Yet families got together for meals, card games, church-related events, and a popular pursuit called "road housing," or alternatively, "honky-tonkin." This form of entertainment was very popular, often rowdy, and did not require significant expense. In addition, children were included, as Richard pointed out. "I went 'road housing' with my parents, and I look back upon that as a really fun time. They would go and dance to the jukebox, drink, and talk. The kids would get Cokes and food—and sometimes a sip of beer or whiskey—and at bedtime, we would be put to bed in the car ... Parents would take turns watching us until it was time to go home."

Such establishments could be rough. Fights occurred. People were thrown out for bad behavior. However, the entertainment was cheap and provided an outlet for stresses associated with life during the Depression.

Another pastime was a card game called "drink or smell." A bottle of home brew was placed in the center of the table, and the winner of each hand got a "drink," while the others only received a "smell." If you were a good card player, you drank a lot. Although Richard was not a serious drinker, he did indulge from time to time. He often returns to northeast Missouri to meet and have a drink with old friends, many of whom are in nursing homes.

Although Duncans Bridge was small, there was plenty for children to do. Compared to computer games kids enjoy today, Richard and his friends enjoyed a game of marbles. He often tagged along with older boys and his cousins, who gave him his first taste of beer and introduced him to tobacco, ball playing, and swimming in the Salt River. Richard's mother fretted about the danger of swimming or even playing near the river. However, he learned how to swim in the river, and the method validated her concern. "Mom didn't want me to swim in the river because she thought I would drown. I didn't know how to swim, so the older boys had their way of teaching me. The river was deepest at the point where it went under the bridge, and those boys would throw me there. They would let me go under once but pulled me out if I started to go under again. That's how I learned to swim."

According to Richard, nothing serious ever happened to him or his friends while having fun. Boys his age tended to be rowdy, which aptly described Richard. Despite the Depression, Richard seemed to have a typical childhood. He worked on his father's farm as a child, and later, when his parents opened a general store, he serviced cars and pumped gas. He was also responsible for the creamery at the store and delivered groceries to country people who couldn't get to town. He soon realized the poverty among these families, and his parents taught him never to give the impression that he was superior to them in any way. It made an impression that became prominent in his dealings with people throughout life. He came to enjoy the people he visited, including an elderly man who never came to town, often described by local people as odd. Richard, however, came to understand the uniqueness of the man and enjoyed learning about his life experiences. He visited with him often as he made his deliveries, always taking time to listen and talk. Later on, Richard gave him a set of encyclopedias as an expression of appreciation.

One summer during World War II, when most able-bodied men were in the armed forces, young Richard worked as a water boy during the wheat harvest and later as a "shocker." This entailed gathering wheat bundles into piles for the threshing machine. It was during this experience that he first encountered African American men also working on the harvest. According to Richard, they were kind men who looked after him and taught him what to do.

One day Richard joined these men at lunchtime, unaware of the racial differences that kept white and black people apart at that time. The farmer approached and instructed Richard to "go eat with the white workers and not these niggers." His statement was representative of the pervasive discrimination of that period. While Richard complied, the incident left him confused and concerned. To the mind of a child, it didn't seem right. Prior to the Civil War, many Missourians owned slaves, a practice that accompanied the migration from the east. His perspective changed, and as his awareness of racial issues grew, so did his sense of tolerance and compassion for people of color. This experience was one of several experiences that influenced his empathetic nature.

Finding a Sense of Direction

As a teenager, Richard was preoccupied with all the typical adolescent distractions. He enjoyed the ten-mile school bus ride to high school in Clarence, Missouri. Since Duncans Bridge was the origin for the bus route, Richard took particular pleasure in occupying the front seat, where he could tease and harangue everyone else who got on board. As a high school student, he was active in sports, plays, and other school functions. In his senior year, he was involved in several instances of misbehavior that, much to his father's chagrin, resulted in a lengthy suspension from school. His father put him to work on the farm, but Richard enjoyed sleeping late, which led to a rebuke from his father. Richard put it this way: "There was no indoor plumbing in Duncans Bridge, and people who could afford to have their outside toilet cleaned hired someone to do it. There was a community shit house cleaner, and I remember my dad saying, 'Well if you want to clean shit houses for the rest of your life, just stay in bed.' I guess that was advice. He may have given me more advice than I realized—it was his way of motivating me."

The image of the outhouse cleaner was clear: Don't take life seriously, continue to get in trouble at school, and this is how your life will play out. He went further, suggesting that if he didn't make something of himself, he shouldn't plan on the largess of his family for support. The message was a jolt of reality. He was nearing the end of high school and had no plans for what would happen next.

Richard was fond of his vocational agriculture teacher, who encouraged him to consider a career in teaching. He took Richard to visit the University of Missouri, and Richard wanted to enroll, but the cost was financially impossible for his family. Therefore, he decided to pursue a position as a country schoolteacher, which didn't require a college degree. He discussed his interest with his father, a former school board member, who not only encouraged him but also used his connections to assist Richard in getting his first teaching job.

The elder Overfelt accompanied Richard in visiting the various country school boards in the county. In those days, an appointment was not required; you just knocked on the door. Richard appreciated the connections his father helped him make. He began to understand the role of influence in making things happen.

> That's often the way it happens with jobs here. The staff we have hired for Highcroft this year have been brought to me by other people, and I have been influenced by their recommendations. So that experience where my dad helped me to get that job in the country school was the beginning. I'm certain he called in a chit to help me get that job. (Interview, November 1977)

In these times of national teaching standards and state certification requirements, it is difficult to believe that someone could teach without appropriate credentials sanctioned by a state agency. Yet that was the case with Richard Overfelt, barely out of high school. We should remember that at that time, the education of children was carried out in one-room schools, representing more than fifteen hundred school districts strewn across the state. College-trained teachers were the exception, and those with degrees usually found employment in metropolitan areas with higher salaries. Therefore, Richard Overfelt, in need of a job and without any training, began his first assignment at Woodlawn School. He had just turned seventeen!

The Depression exposed people to a wide range of influences, and most were serious in their effect. Figure 1 depicts the relationship among key events. In the small insular community of Duncans Bridge, Richard was shielded from some of the most difficult aspects of the Depression by his parents, who were recognized for their work ethic and outreach to others who were less fortunate. They were loath to watch his every activity, largely because of the need to work for a living. Within the rather cloistered atmosphere of Duncans Bridge, Richard had a degree of freedom to make choices about recreation. His parents provided a supportive atmosphere but held high expectations for appropriate behavior.

When Richard started working in the wheat harvest and later at the family store, he encountered the ugliness of racial discrimination and an awareness of the extreme poverty among country people outside Duncans Bridge. The combination of negative aspects of the Depression and exposure to family values influenced the psychological differentiation that leads to the true self. Robert Firestone (2012) has written extensively about differentiation as a process people experience in shaping identity. I don't believe Richard was aware of the fine points of the process in his transition from boyhood to adult, but through the help of parents and others, he began to think about negative environmental aspects as he matured.

As Firestone pointed out, differentiation is a lifelong process that leads to one's true self.

Over time, Richard developed a sense of empathy. Exposure to the enterprising work ethic of his parents, in addition to their sense of responsibility and positive criticism, helped to shape his sense of direction beyond high school.

His father's timely assistance in securing his first teaching position and the advice he gave Richard along the way were important lessons he never forgot. From the time he was a young boy, he possessed a good sense of humor, a strategic quality helpful in working collaboratively with people.

Finally, through a gradual process of differentiation during a period of significant strife, Richard became determined to make something of himself.

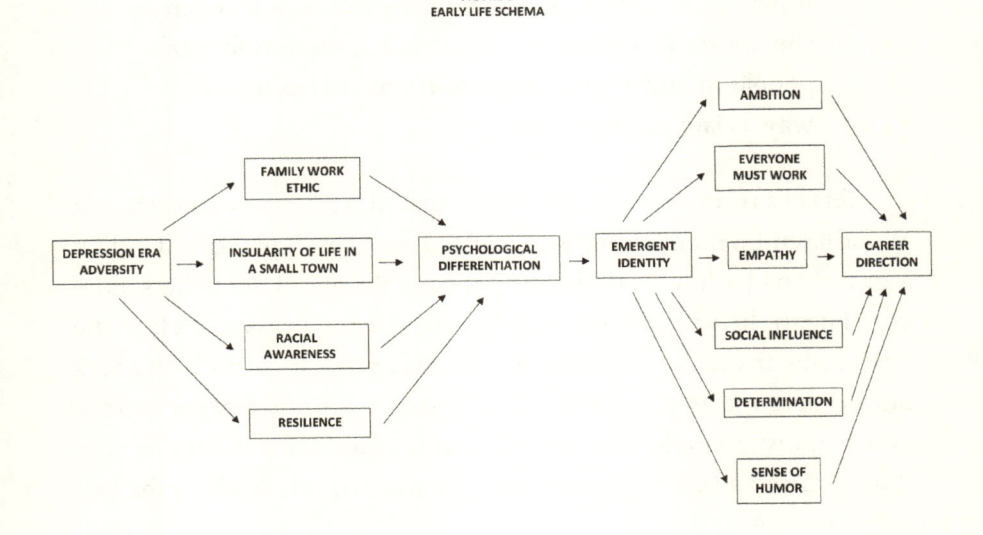

FIGURE 1
EARLY LIFE SCHEMA

Teaching in a One-Room Country School

Country schools were a sharp contrast to present-day schools. It is difficult to grasp the circumstances impacting the life and work of teachers in those country schools. There were, of course, no unions, maintenance personnel, or subject matter specialists to support their work. It was a unique time, and teachers had much to shoulder. Studs Terkel (1986), a keen observer of the Depression era, offered his personal experience:

> I went to an old country-style schoolhouse ... one building that had eight rows in it, one for each grade. Seven rows were quiet, while the eighth row recited. The woman teacher got the munificent sum of thirty dollars a month. She played the pump organ, taught every subject in all eight grades ... At the back corner was a great potbellied stove that kept the place warm. The school was on about an acre and had a playground with no equipment. Out there were toilets, three-holers, with moon crescents or stars on the doors. You would be surprised at the number of people in rural areas who didn't have much in this way as late as the 1930s.

Terkel's recollections mirrored much of Richard's experience at Woodlawn Elementary School, located on a small parcel of land on a gravel road a few miles from Duncans Bridge. Before the school year began, he was given ten dollars to cut the grass and clear the tree limbs from the playground. He was not happy with the task but accepted it as part of the job. Today a groundskeeper with a power mower would do this task, but Richard used a hand scythe that required a full day to complete. It was tedious work in the late summer heat.

Preparing the school building followed. He cleaned the inside and applied cylinder oil to the floor to abate dust and dirt. Then came the sacks of lime, one for the outside toilets to mitigate odor and another for the well to purify the water. In short, as a country schoolteacher,

Richard taught children, provided custodial services, collected wood for the stove, and was ever observant for unannounced visits by the county superintendent.

He was seventeen when he began teaching in August 1946 with no formal training, which was often the norm for country schools. He had a great deal to learn. Richard again turned to his father, who offered advice.

> He reviewed me on how to figure the number of bushels in a wagonload of corn ... how to figure the depth of a well and how much water the thing would hold. He said someone from the community would stop by. No one ever asked me to figure the amount of water in the well, but one day a farmer pulled up that road [gesturing to the portrait of Woodlawn School on the office wall] and asked me if I would come out and help him know how much corn was in that wagon. That was a little test.

Last in the Box

Country schools were often the site of community social activities. Richard's father told him that his first exposure to community judgment would be at a pie (or box) supper, where girls prepared boxed meals that were auctioned off to the highest bidder as everyone watched to see which girl was most popular. But in Richard's view, the excitement of the event was diminished when a box supper was not sold, resulting in a girl eating alone. Richard sensed the humiliation she must have experienced, and he coined the phrase "last in the box" to describe it. It means someone who is consciously or unconsciously left out, unrecognized.

He recalled that he felt like a last in the box kid in high school because he was from the country. Country kids were obvious because they wore bibbed overalls, while town kids wore jeans.

He remembered how much he wanted a pair, and he tried to fit in by adapting his bibbed overalls to look like jeans. Bibbed overalls had shoulder straps he rearranged around his waist, and he folded the bibbed part under his shirt to create the impression that he was wearing jeans. Trying to fit in was difficult when you are viewed as different, an oddity.

His memories included instances of hazing, when he and other country kids were taken to the local cemetery, tied to tombstones, and abandoned. Something similar happened when he began taking college classes offered specifically for country schoolteachers in the late spring each year. The full-time students immediately noticed the arrival of country schoolteachers on campus, and Richard couldn't help noticing their stares. He had empathy for people who were last in the box, those who were different, like the African American workers during the wheat harvest.

Whether the underlying circumstances were real or imagined, the concept of last in the box remained with him over the years and reappeared during a staff meeting at Highcroft more than thirty years later. Richard passed around a box containing one chocolate for teachers to examine. The room was silent as the box moved through the group while he spoke about the importance of recognizing the value of every student under their care. That's what a "good person" would do, not let anyone fall through the cracks, find ways to make all students feel welcome, valued, and included. Richard was an underdog and never forgot what it was like. It is not far-fetched to say that he was a champion of underdogs.

Developing Credibility

His experiences as a last in the box kid found expression in his work over the years. With continued study and experience, his beliefs about children and teaching matured. He began to understand the relationship between the school and community and the teacher's role in organizing community events. His father was influential in shaping the basic skills required of a country schoolteacher. He told Richard that his ability to organize and lead school activities would be judged by the community, and he took steps to educate Richard on managing school plays and other events to ensure a positive community response. He said, "Make sure that the kids that are not on stage are quiet because the people will listen for that. If the kids backstage are making noise while the kids on stage are giving their recitations, they will think that you are not a good disciplinarian." (Interview, 1977)

Today this sort of practical advice is usually dispensed by a school principal, a mentor, or a colleague. However, in the isolated country schools of that period, where the county superintendent might visit once a year, there was no one to give immediate advice and assistance. Richard's father filled this void with his experience as a board member and his knowledge of the community and its expectations.

Richard recalled the first time the county superintendent came to observe him teach. One needs to understand a teacher's reaction to an impending visit, usually unannounced, and the anxiety it created. But teachers were creative and found a way to alert each other that the superintendent was on her way. Country schools lacked much in terms of equipment, but every school had a telephone. As soon as the superintendent left one school, the teacher would alert others about a pending visit. On one occasion, the superintendent observed Richard teach a history lesson with fifth graders. However, when the superintendent debriefed the lesson, she told him he was using an eighth-grade text.

He said, "I didn't know the difference. What I thought was that those kids were not good readers or that the book was just hard to read. I didn't think I might have had them in the wrong book. That was my first experience with supervision." (Interview, November 1977)

This episode highlights the steep learning curve that Richard faced. To be minimally qualified, a country schoolteacher had to demonstrate subject matter competency annually, and Richard often had to repeat the examinations. One remedy was in the form of workshops and short courses in specific subject matter areas, offered by the county district or college extension. For instance, if the English examination wasn't passed, a teacher could take a class, and if successful, he was exempted from the exam. He earned nine hundred dollars that first year and began formal education studies for a BS degree at Northeast Missouri State College (now Truman State University).

Becoming Aware of Personal and Professional Worth

Richard was not timid when it came to fair compensation. Early in his experience at Woodlawn, he refused to sign a contract unless the salary was higher. When an increase was not forthcoming, he informed the superintendent of his intent to interview with other districts. Upon receipt of a better offer from another district, Richard proceeded to inform his superintendent, who responded with a counteroffer of an additional fifty dollars. He accepted and remained at Woodlawn another year. However, there was a backstory in this episode that reflected existing attitudes regarding women and the way they were paid.

Richard's wife, Myra, was also a country schoolteacher in a nearby district at the time of his contract dispute at Woodlawn. Myra had received a contract for more money than Richard, and he was adamant that his wife should not make more money than he did. This became the underlying reason for his contractual actions at Woodlawn. His reaction was unusual given his sensitivity for people who were different, left out, denigrated for what they wore, their skin color, or their point of origin—and likely a reflection of discriminatory attitudes that existed at the time. Richard later admitted his reaction was inconsistent with his beliefs, especially regarding the equality of women.

By taking college extension courses offered by the county, several five-week semesters during April, referred to as "short springs," and a full year of full-time study, Richard completed his degree. With their bachelor's degrees and experience behind them, Richard and Myra looked beyond Duncans Bridge to new horizons in education.

Upon return from military service during the Korean conflict, Richard completed his MA degree, and he and Myra began teaching in Keokuk, Iowa. Along with his teaching responsibilities, Richard also worked as elementary curriculum director.

After a few years in Keokuk, Richard accepted an elementary principal position at the Kirkwood School District in suburban St. Louis. While there, he was appointed assistant superintendent for elementary education. District patrons appreciated his positive, friendly manner in working with people. He was recognized for the way he found solutions to difficult issues, and several parents began a campaign to have him appointed superintendent. Along the way, Richard completed the PhD in education administration at St. Louis University and began to consider what he really wanted to do.

Richard enjoyed working with children and teachers, and although the role of assistant superintendent was important, it did not satisfy his interest in school-based leadership. His aspirations were realized when he accepted a position as principal of Riverbend Elementary School in the Parkway School District in 1972. Five years later, he was appointed principal of Highcroft Ridge Elementary School, which was in the initial stages of planning. Also in 1972, Richard became an adjunct professor of education at Truman State University and Lincoln University, teaching a variety of graduate courses for experienced teachers. Amid accolades from his students, he has served in this position for more than forty years.

Summary

Richard grew up during a time of significant challenge for most Americans. The Depression framed all aspects of life in the 1930s, when small, rural farmers struggled to maintain their farms. Franklin Roosevelt's New Deal eventually improved conditions, but serious conflict continued to exist among large versus small farmers who competed for meager federal assistance. It took years to rectify the problem, and many farms simply failed. It was only through individual enterprise and adaptability that Richard's family succeeded. As a youth, he was exposed to the strong work ethic of his mother and father, who believed that work would eventually lead him to a self-sufficient life. Figure 2 highlights elements leading to Richard's career in education.

Largely due to his father's intervention, Richard began having serious thought about how he would support himself after high school. His thinking was magnified by paternal expectations that he would have to support himself and, at some point, not rely on his family. He was young but had some work experience, and due to the

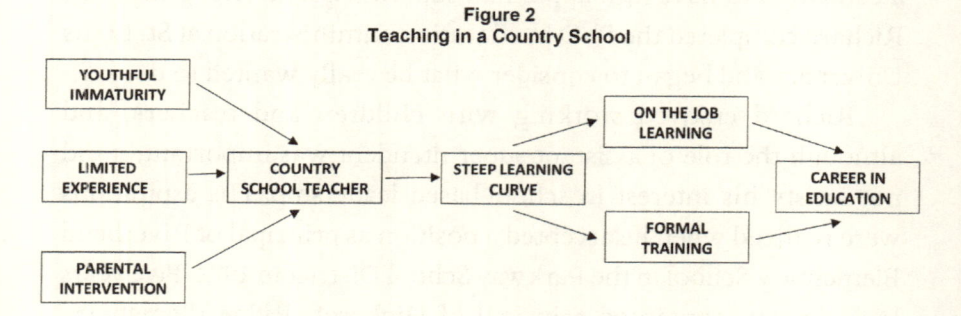

Figure 2
Teaching in a Country School

YOUTHFUL IMMATURITY → COUNTRY SCHOOL TEACHER
LIMITED EXPERIENCE → COUNTRY SCHOOL TEACHER
PARENTAL INTERVENTION → COUNTRY SCHOOL TEACHER
COUNTRY SCHOOL TEACHER → STEEP LEARNING CURVE
STEEP LEARNING CURVE → ON THE JOB LEARNING → CAREER IN EDUCATION
STEEP LEARNING CURVE → FORMAL TRAINING → CAREER IN EDUCATION

advice of a favorite teacher, he became a teacher in a country school. He had some inside help from his father, who called in a chit in helping him with his first position. Richard was a novice but had determination and organizational skills fundamental to the work of a teacher, which is best described as "learning on the job."

He learned to take competency tests required by the county superintendent and classes made available to country schoolteachers. In the early stages of his career, he relied on his father's practical advice as a member of the board of education. Visits from the superintendent were infrequent but useful in correcting errors of instruction.

For all Richard's strengths as a person, he was acutely aware of attitudes or opinions others may have—directly or indirectly—made about him and his origins in Duncans Bridge. As a country kid, he was sometimes the target of hazing incidents during high school. When he attended college classes on campus during short spring sessions, he noticed the denigrating looks he sometime received from full-time students. His gradual understanding of racial and class differences influenced the concept he called "last in the box." This influenced his sensitivity for people who were judged to be different and unacceptable due to their race, ethnicity, or place of origin. These factors were prominent in his development of empathy. He understood what it was like to be an underdog. His empathic understanding of people of all stripes was characteristic of his leadership throughout the course of his long career.

CHAPTER 3
Research Methods

Ethnography

A few words about research methods used in writing this book are important to understanding outcomes. The study originated during the course of graduate work in 1980, but due to the realities of family and profession, time was not conducive to writing a book. But now in retirement, more time became available to complete the project that began so many years ago.

My research interests were closely aligned with certification as a secondary school administrator. Previous experiences as a biology teacher, science department chairman, and later, director of the St. Louis Metropolitan Teacher Center were important as a foundation that eventually led to a career in school administration. As a science teacher, I understood standard research and the use of statistics in gathering and interpreting data. I had extensive experience with science research in studying plant and animal systems but sought a methodology more favorable to understanding human organizations like schools. Consequently, I utilized a range of techniques commonly found within the field of ethnography.

Ethnographers, like anthropologists, seek to understand phenomena through immersion in natural systems. As a researcher, one derives data through close observations of members of a group as they go about their daily lives. More specifically, the role is referred to as "participant observation," where the observer occupies a continuum of involvement with complete detachment to an active participant. In reality, both extremes are utilized in collecting and interpreting data regarding work, relationship patterns, rituals and sentiments, and related domains to observe and interpret the character of a culture. It is for these reasons that participant observation was used to study a principal and staff engaged in planning a new organization. I was especially interested in how a principal worked with teachers to develop a sense of collaboration in shaping the culture of a school.

Origins of the Study

The study began after meeting Dr. Richard Overfelt soon after he was appointed principal of Highcroft Ridge Elementary School in the Parkway School District in suburban St. Louis. He was responsible for preparations required to open the school in August 1978. My initial discussion with Richard (he eschewed formal titles) revealed his intent to begin meeting with recently hired staff in January to begin planning. We discussed my interest in a research study of his school, beginning with planning sessions in January, the opening of school in August, and into the first year of operation. He subsequently approved the plan, which also received school district approval.

In the most general sense, the research problem involved issues related to the development of a new school. I was curious about the planning sessions and how the leadership of the principal and teachers would be manifested. I wondered how teachers would acclimate to shared decision-making among grade-level teams and the development of trust and positive relationships integral to effective collaboration. Similarly, I was interested in Richard's background and the extent that early life experience was influential in his work at Highcroft.

Sources of Data

As a participant observer, I devoted several hundred hours with Richard and his staff during the planning phase, the opening of school, and through the school year. Like an anthropologist, a participant observer employs multiple methods of data collection, including direct observation, formal and informal interviews, and the collection of artifacts.

Observations of planning sessions, classroom teaching, meetings, and school activities were handwritten, coded, and organized as field notes. Interviews with Richard, teachers, and parents were often scheduled, tape-recorded, and transcribed for further analysis. Informal conversations were also entered in field notes, and a variety of documents were collected and examined. These included staff meeting agendas, minutes of meetings, school handbooks, personal and professional communications, and school district curriculum guides. These sources led to the discovery of multiple variables in the planning and implementation of a school. The resulting "triangulation" (Denzin 1970) of multiple data sources is critical to achieving concrete understanding of complex events. Glaser and Strauss (1967) have argued that this approach is important in developing grounded theory. Abraham Maslow (1965) summarized the stance of the participant observer accurately: "He doesn't design, control, manipulate, or change anything. Ultimately, he is simply a non-interfering observer and a good reporter." His characterization became the standard for my work as researcher.

The investigation initially focused on Richard, his early history at Duncans Bridge, and his plans for the new school. Attending the first staff meeting in January 1978 was another step in the process, followed by monthly staff meetings between February and August. As a participant observer, I was present for the majority of formal and informal events during the year. In their investigation of a new innovative elementary school, Smith and Keith (1971) proposed an organizational framework consisting of preliminary phases, attending to details of data collection, and final analysis, and writing to guide their progress. My work was aligned with the procedures they suggested.

The Organizational Plan of the Book

Chapters 1 and 2 create a biographical sketch of Richard's early life and his evolution as a teacher in a small one-room school. Chapters 4 through 11 discuss the processes involved in the organizational development of Highcroft Elementary School through the 1978 school year. Chapter 12 juxtaposes the results of the study with the larger body of research on school development and leadership. Finally, an Epilogue discusses the findings from the five-year follow-up study, along with final thoughts and reflections.

The culmination of the research, reflection, and writing is a story about a man with humble beginnings who progressed from teaching in a one-room country school to elementary school principal, adjunct professor of education, and recognition as a leader in public education.

CHAPTER 4
Planning a New School

The Architecture of an Open-Plan School

Following World War II, a new instructional approach emerged in Britain that changed the way pupils were taught. The open classroom method emphasized learning by doing, where pupils were actively involved in learning. This approach was in contrast to the teacher-centered approaches typical of most schools in the early twentieth century. In the United States, schools had been subjected to attacks by critics, blaming them for everything from the Russian Sputnik to urban deterioration. They were criticized for not developing enough engineers and scientists, for being racially segregated, lacking in outreach to disadvantaged children, and for producing uncreative graduates who seldom questioned authority. In the 1950s, critics blamed schools for creating a culture of conformity, accusing teacher-led classroom instruction for crushing student creativity.

In the United States, open classrooms influenced the trend toward open-space architectural planning. As teaching began to shift in the direction of active learning, the historic view of fixed boxlike classrooms gave way to more flexible space favoring multiple activities where the teacher provided guidance and assistance rather than direct instruction. Schools with open arrangements appeared in the 1960s and were not always well received by parents.

Highcroft was located on eighteen acres in a new subdivision on the western end of the school district. It was populated by young largely professional and upwardly mobile families. The interior of the school was nontraditional (see figure 3). Individual classroom spaces were replaced by pods staffed by four teachers in grade levels one through six and two teachers in kindergarten. Pods were arranged along the outside perimeter of the building along a U-shaped hallway, with low walls separating the pods from the passage. Thus one could walk the length of the hall along pods three and four, turn right facing pods five and six, and turn right again along pods two, three, and kindergarten with visual access throughout.

Pods were separated by project areas containing drinking fountains, restrooms and storage, and alternative space for small group instruction. The grades within a pod could be separated into four classrooms by a flexible curtain as needed by instructional plans of teaching teams. The Learning Resource Center (LRC) was in the middle of the building, with convenient access to all the pods. It too was bounded by a low wall, permitting an unobstructed view from end to end. A quiet reading area called "the cave" was located in an alcove on the east end of the LRC, where the librarian had placed an old bathtub outfitted with stuffed animals. Teacher workspaces, LRC resources, and equipment storage occupied the opposite end of the LRC.

Offices for principal, counselor, nurse, and support staff, a small meeting area ("rocking chair room"), gym, and multipurpose area that doubled as a cafeteria were located on the west end, near the main entrance. Classrooms for special use—like music, art, and special education—and the teacher's lunchroom and the kitchen completed the internal space. The training sessions initiated by Richard were largely intended to engage teachers in planning a system of instruction for the unique open environment. The significance of planning was heightened by the fact that no one on the staff had direct experience with open-plan schools. It was simultaneously daunting and exhilarating as the staff worked together on the design of a program from the ground up.

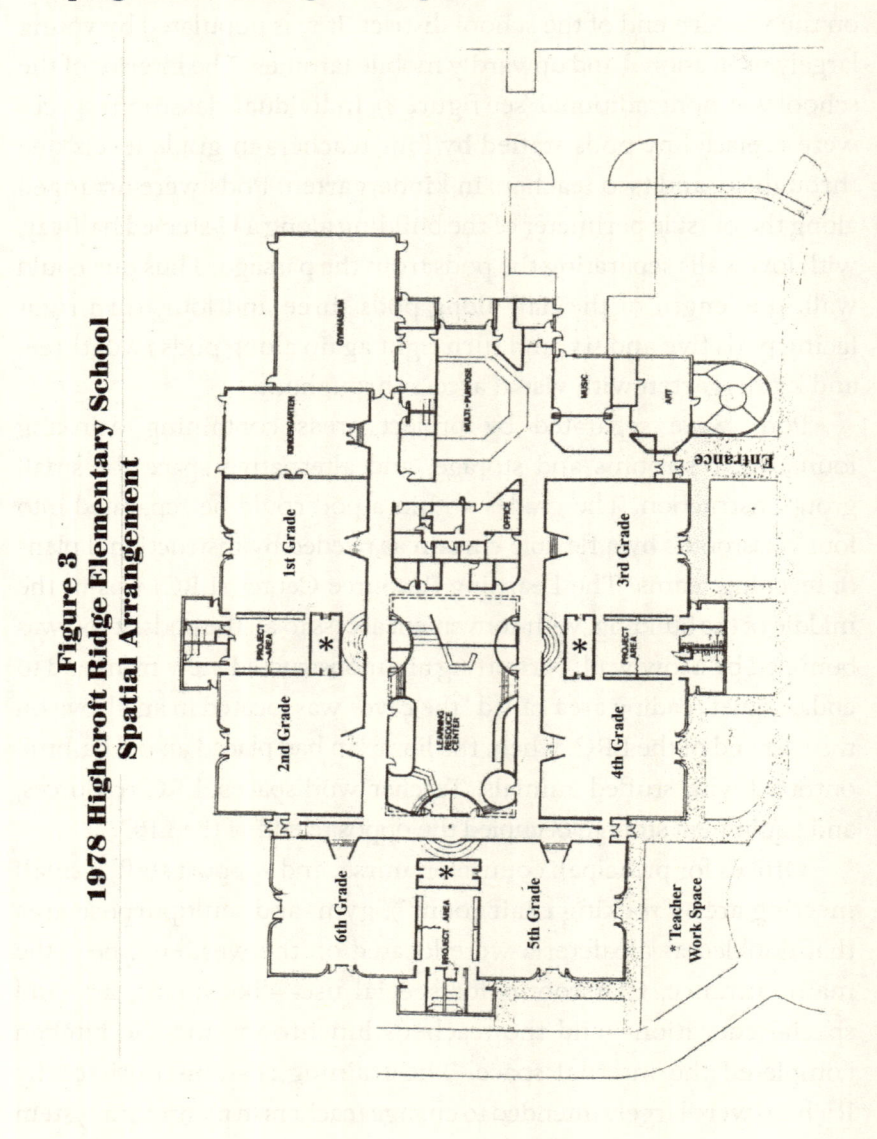

Figure 3
1978 Highcroft Ridge Elementary School
Spatial Arrangement

Educational Change: A Familiar but Complex Process

Planning and implementing a new school is an example of educational change. Change in any form occurs first in the minds of people who are directly involved, and although it sounds simple enough, change is a complex process. To understand this concept, imagine a time that you were learning to ride a bicycle, pedaling slowly and carefully, perhaps enjoying the expansive feeling of movement under your control. Gaining confidence, you pedaled faster, and in your peripheral vision, you noticed a ball rolling in your direction. It was obviously going to collide with your bicycle. You began to lose your balance and poise and quickly swerved, applied the brake, and avoided the ball. It worked! Your ability to adapt prevented an accident, and your sense of control returned. You learned from the experience and could predict what would happen next: a return to steadiness and continued progress. The change was not the sudden appearance of the ball but your ability to adapt cognitively to changing conditions.

Educational change often follows a linear process of decision-making under the guidance of a leader. This is also referred to as a "top-down" approach, where participants act on directives from a leader. Teachers, for example, are usually on the receiving end of directives and carry out actual implementation of plans. However, in recent years, we have learned from mathematics and science that natural systems are often "self-organizing" and occur in a manner quite different from a linear approach to change. This raises many questions currently being discussed in the literature on educational change. One wonders how a change may occur without centralized control and management. In social systems, such as schools with multiple participants, how are decisions made? It is obvious that one person will find it very difficult to control the thoughts and actions of group members. So what does it mean to be in a system that organizes itself? Without going into the complexity involved, perhaps a hypothetical example will promote understanding.

Imagine an elementary school experiencing declining enrollment and its continuing existence is in question. In an earlier time, the school served a largely middle-class community, but in recent years, the area had experienced changes in basic services, homes that fell into disrepair, and an increase in vandalism. The principal and her assistant were concerned about the impact of declining enrollment and a possible decision by the board of education to close the school. The principals reacted by encouraging teachers to continue the existing curriculum and examine what other schools did in similar situations. There was a great deal of concern among the staff as many began to consider their professional futures.

Conversations among individuals and small groups of teachers began to occur, and several ideas rose to a higher level of discussion among the entire staff. A few teachers began to discuss ways to tighten up the existing curriculum and work harder to reach students. Others had been talking about the disparity of the current curriculum and the needs of their changing enrollment. They recognized that many students required more focused attention not currently available in the self-contained classroom arrangement at the school. As the level of interaction increased around these ideas, a workable idea surfaced: would it be possible to use the old gymnasium as an alternative learning site that could assess and plan activities for students who were underachieving?

The dialogue increased to the point where teachers proposed their idea to the administration. Principals listened and saw merit in their plan, and together they set out to install new learning opportunities for disadvantaged children.

The example is purely hypothetical but likely a common occurrence in large cities today. I encourage the reader to focus on the process rather than the substance of the example. In the beginning, there was a serious change in the community, with a direct impact on school function. The principals recognized the issues and tried to stimulate discussion in the direction they chose.

The teachers also recognized pending difficulty and were concerned about the future. In the language of complexity theory (Berreby 1996), this is called the emergence of a "disequilibrium" and the creation of "uncertainty." Conditions are changing. What can be done? What should we do?

Individuals and small groups began thinking about possible interventions, and their interactions began to reach the greater number of staff who grasped an idea that all could accept, including the administration. They created a sufficient disequilibrium by disrupting existing patterns of thought and action.

All change follows a similar pattern. Disequilibrium leads to uncertainty, some form of disruption followed by interactions, first among dyads, then small groups, and then among the totality of participants. Complexity resides in the degree and quality of interaction as it relates to the need for change. Administrators are not passive bystanders in educational change. They need to support effective deliberations, ease the momentum toward disequilibrium in order to facilitate pervasive interaction, support teachers, and avoid the tendency to impose a decision of their own liking.

Temporary Systems: A Training Model

When Richard was appointed as principal in 1977, he began thinking about staff training that would eventually lead to the opening of school. It was an immense task requiring extended days of training. The design of a social system consistent with flexible space of an open-plan school required significant adaptation by everyone. All staff members brought their previous experiences and preconceived ideas to the process, and much of what they were accustomed to would need to be modified, if not cast aside. Richard gave considerable thought to a training format that would ease the transformation.

When members of a group consider the kinds of institutions they have frequented, most tend to recall long-lasting permanent structures. The university, a corporation, a family group, a community agency, and the army are all are forms of organizational structures with long lives that people expect to exist indefinitely, outlasting participation by individuals. Most of the inquiry into human social organization has focused on arrangements considered permanent and durable.

However, in reflecting on the virtues of permanent systems, we are aware of a large number of "temporary systems" (Miles 1964) that at some point in time will cease to exist. These include conventions, task forces, religious retreats, and professional development programs. In the case of Highcroft Ridge, a temporary system became the means for reeducating teachers for participation in team planning and teaching.

For several reasons, permanent systems (organizations, persons, or groups) find it hard to change themselves. Within these systems, most of the existing energy is invested in maintaining organizational routines. Typically, the time and energy required for planning and implementing new innovations in an established school is limited. Thus the system of meetings in Richard's plan were intended to separate participants, at least partially, from their existing work in order to focus on detailed planning of Highcroft. The desired outcome rested heavily on reeducation of all involved: teachers, pupils, parents, and staff.

In my view, the utilization of systematic planning procedures was essential to socialization of teachers and others on the staff. The opening of a new school, with all its varied elements, represents a change in structure and format experienced by new members of the school. Years ago, in the middle of the last century, Kurt Lewin (1951) developed a conceptual scheme about social change that sharpens our understanding of how socialization occurs. Most importantly, socialization involves a change in existing behavior to meet the requirements of a new social system. Lewin used commonsense language to point out that social change involves a process of "unfreezing," "moving" (adapting), and "refreezing" of new group standards. Lewin suggested that "unfreezing," or dissolution of previous group standards, is supported by three interacting factors.

The first consists of a marked emotional reaction or catharsis that loosens the grasp of established standards of behavior. Second, working in isolation with other members of a group creates, in Lewin's terms, a "cultural island" where new ideas, unencumbered by the past, can be safely considered. Third, the ultimate result is a new group coming together to establish plans. The Highcroft planning sessions exposed participants to these elements, and because participants are often at different points in this scheme, movement toward a new social system is best described as a gradualist process of refreezing of new standards.

The efficacy of temporary systems like the Highcroft planning team in changing patterns of thinking and conduct depends largely on the creation of isolation or cultural islands during a period of change. The stronger the attitudes of participants for adapting existing behavior and the more isolated it is can reduce resistance among individual participants and smooth the pathway to emerging group standards.

The First Staff Meeting

On the evening of January 23, 1978, fresh snow had fallen. I could feel the crunch underfoot as I made my way up the steps to the district office building. When I entered the boardroom, I noticed that Richard had arranged chairs in an oval around the perimeter. He greeted each arrival with a hug or handshake, along with smiles and laughter, as he recollected past experiences. Richard was of average height and build, and he was dressed in a white shirt and matching tie. He was completely at ease and seemed to enjoy all the exchanges with teachers and staff. Several teachers had brought food, and they conversed with each other around the refreshment table. The pleasantness of the early minutes put everyone at ease as the formal meeting began.

Thirty-seven of the forty-one staff members were present. Richard explained that some had prior commitments and would be present at the February meeting. It was noteworthy that one teacher on each grade-level team had previously worked with Richard at Riverbend School, which provided a core of leadership at Highcroft Ridge.

Among the professional staff, sixteen teachers were new to the district, while six knew him previously. Seven teachers had been hired in 1976 and placed in other district elementary schools, then transferred to Highcroft the following year. Some of these teachers were placed in schools with children who would attend Highcroft, thereby providing a familiar link between children and teachers. Twenty-seven teachers were female, and six were male. In addition to teachers, several secretaries, a few aides, the school nurse, and supervisor of custodians were also present.

Richard took particular pains in identifying teachers for Highcroft. Teachers remembered their interviews as something they had never experienced in the past. One teacher's account of her interview was typical of remarks made by other staff members: "When I interviewed with Richard, it was the most interesting thing I had ever gone through. It was three hours long! Before the interview, I thought he would want to know about curricula I had taught. He couldn't have cared less what reading or math series I used. He wanted to know what kind of person I was, how I was going to work with young children, and what others would say about me as a person. That revealed a lot about how he works. He is the most tremendous person I've ever worked for. I have never worked with a principal like Richard."

Beliefs as an Expression of Formal Doctrine

In their study of an innovative elementary school, Smith and Keith (1971) described the various perspectives contributing to the "formal doctrine" of an organization. In their view, formal doctrine contains elements that are visionary and visible in organizational documents and day-to-day communications. It contains an elaborated system of concepts describing the operating structure within an organization.

The "institutional plan" was another concept identified by Smith and Keith, representing formal doctrine that described essentials of the instructional program from the principal's point of view. In their study, the institutional plan was codified in a document written by the principal, outlining a unique program of individualized instruction. At Highcroft, elements of formal doctrine, institutional plan, goals, and beliefs could be found in Richard's paper, "Planning for a New School," and especially in his introductory remarks at the first staff meeting.

Richard began to describe the kind of school he hoped Highcroft would become. In general terms, it was his institutional plan for the new school. Teachers were exposed to it during interviews and now as a starting point for the entire staff as planning began. Everyone gave close attention to his lengthy introduction:

> Today we and our children face a world that changes each second, a world that will make unknown demands on our children. The only way we can honestly prepare them to live in and cope with that world is to provide them with the basic tools. Our pupils will learn how to learn. They will not only know how to read; they will want to read. They will not only know how to compute; they will understand the system of computation and be able to apply it to all kinds of problem solving situations. They will not only know how to write, spell, and punctuate; they will know how to communicate—to reach out to their fellow man and talk to him, and listen to him, and try to understand him.

Our pupils will respect human differences; they will appreciate and value those differences. Today, as we see the world shrink to the point where anything that happens affects all of us, it is important that our children learn to value the diversity of mankind. We can only ask our children to respect differences in others if we respect their own differences. We cannot treat our children as numbers on achievement curves and then ask them to be positive, constructive individuals. We cannot separate the classroom from the world and then expect our children to apply what they have learned to their lives. Our pupils will become self-directed human beings. They will internalize a value system that is human and humane, and they will act in concert with that system throughout life. (Meeting minutes, 1/23/78)

It was an astonishing oration of beliefs, values, and goals. Everyone was attentive and some took notes. Richard's presentation had the solemnity of a church service. His remarks were presented in a slow, clear cadence, in a style reminiscent of a country preacher delivering a sermon. He was relaxed, his voice somewhat folksy, with just a hint of an accent, typical of rural folks in Northeast Missouri farm country.

His opening salvo covered a lot of ground about the role of education as preparation for life, including respect for diversity, a positive work ethic, and the need for teachers to respect students. Teaching is not a sterile activity without connection to the world. Richard's ultimate goal was to prepare students for life in a complex world. However, in the main, his remarks were an expression of the Highcroft Ridge formal doctrine summarized in figure 4. Elements of the doctrine also connected with values teachers have for nurturing children. As the meeting progressed, Richard paused to express his excitement about the journey they were about to begin, saying, "It's a moment I have been preparing for all my life."

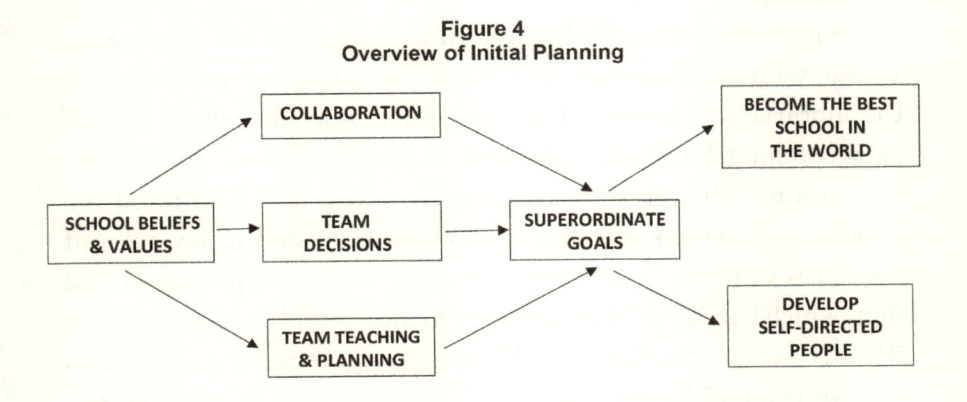

Figure 4
Overview of Initial Planning

```
                    COLLABORATION                      BECOME THE BEST
                   ↗             ↘                     SCHOOL IN
                  ↗               ↘                 ↗  THE WORLD
 SCHOOL BELIEFS →  TEAM         →  SUPERORDINATE
   & VALUES        DECISIONS       GOALS
                  ↘               ↗                 ↘  DEVELOP
                   ↘             ↗                     SELF-DIRECTED
                    TEAM TEACHING                      PEOPLE
                    & PLANNING
```

The meeting was briefly interrupted by the arrival of the assistant superintendent for elementary education, who commented on the importance of advance planning. He encouraged them in their task and presented anticipated enrollment data for the Highcroft attendance area, where the final sixty homes were under construction. As he concluded his remarks, Richard stated that he was a friend of Highcroft Elementary School and thanked him for his support. A bit later, the superintendent arrived to recognize the importance of their planning, and he also expressed appreciation for their effort. Comments from these key administrators suggested that Highcroft held special status as a "protected subculture" within the school district.

Steps in Building a Staff

Richard introduced staff members, asking each to briefly share something about them. This was met by smiles and anticipation as each spoke. Some were more verbose than others were, but everyone listened as each shared a good deal about their beliefs, training, and experience. They were going to be a team and seemed eager to understand their cohorts. The process required more time than expected, and Richard appeared a bit nervous as he moved the agenda along.

One staff member had taught in a country school. Most were young, with limited experience. A few had ten-plus years, including the librarian, a seasoned professional, who described herself as a teaching librarian interested in working with teachers on curriculum. All were effusive in their praise of Richard and the opportunity to work with him and others in the group. Several staff members were recommended to him by teachers who were hired first, which hearkened back to the influence his father had in helping Richard secure his first teaching position. Everything seemed to revolve around Richard, who sat smiling, occasionally making jokes, creating a positive atmosphere as the meeting unfolded.

The Good Person Ethic

The focus of the meeting continued as Richard began to discuss a significant goal: "Highcroft will be the best school in the world in two to three years," and "This staff is the best, maybe not technically but as persons." He quickly clarified the latter point: "The staff is excellent, but being a good person is important in working with children." This was followed by an admonition: "Support your school and colleagues. Leave problems and arguments at school." Revealed in the opening moments of the meeting, these points seemed to indicate one of Richard's core values: technical skills were important, but being a good person was critical. A few teachers who'd worked with him in the past or knew him socially had one thing in common: long interviews of two hours or more that focused on their human qualities and beliefs about children. Considerably less time was given to matters of curriculum and teaching.

He continued: "Children become much of what the teacher is. I am a teacher, positive not negative. Teachers become what they perceive themselves to be. If I hurt someone through negativism,

I lose something of myself; good breeds good. We are the *they*. We must be models for children."

In my experience as a teacher, attending more staff meetings than I can remember, I never heard opening remarks such as these. I was used to a welcome, introductions, a review of the school manual, and updates of board of education policies. Richard's remarks were more philosophical, oriented toward things he valued and hoped to live by as leader: be positive and recognize the importance of working as a community and expectations for being the best person possible. Further, as he expanded upon values, he revealed himself as a human being intent on achieving the best outcomes for teachers and students (figure 5).

> I want to be a good person, keep things simple, and count my blessings. I want to be reasonable, available, and decisive. It is OK to make mistakes: me, teachers, and kids. I will try not to fuss about the appearance of the building [but admitted that would be hard during inclement weather]. I will try not to talk at teachers and promise not to get on teachers when they are down. I won't ask people who are thoughtful to do thoughtful things.

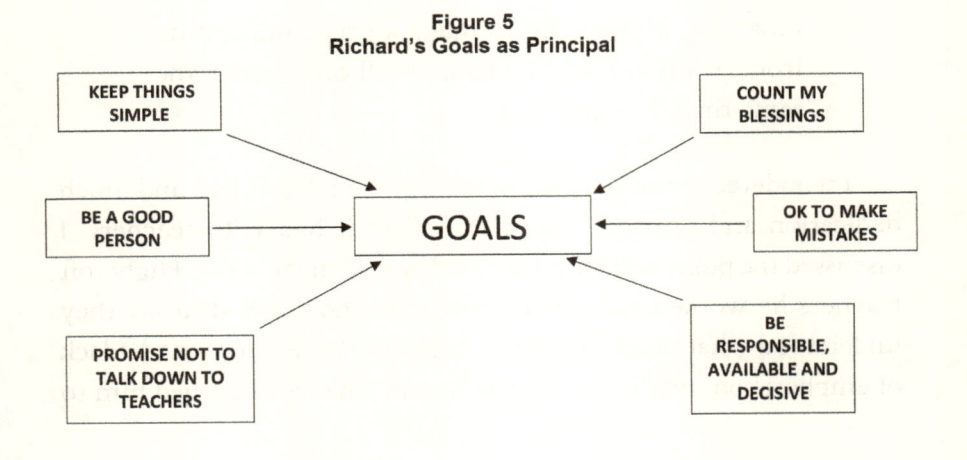

**Figure 5
Richard's Goals as Principal**

- KEEP THINGS SIMPLE
- COUNT MY BLESSINGS
- BE A GOOD PERSON
- OK TO MAKE MISTAKES
- PROMISE NOT TO TALK DOWN TO TEACHERS
- BE RESPONSIBLE, AVAILABLE AND DECISIVE

→ GOALS

Everything he spoke about to this point was concerned with human attributes he associated with "good persons" and effective teaching. The practical matters of curriculum, classroom management, and instructional materials were to be addressed in later meetings. He was interested in building trust and positive working relationships he viewed critical to teaching in an open-plan school. His focus then shifted to expectations for teachers who would help shape the school culture.

> Be good persons; you are all known quantities. Work hard. I am willing to go with less talent and much dedication and purpose because this produces winners. Be on time [adding that he explored this thoroughly during interviews]. It boggles my mind when people are late[he expected teachers to put in whatever time was necessary and not merely guided by 20 minutes before and after school typical of teacher contracts] Do we have respect for each other on this? [A teacher commented that this was important, and several others nodded their heads in agreement.] I don't want to be mean about this but would rather let people go if it was a problem. Be a self-starter; have confidence. No bitching or moaning. If you want to make a gripe, make it up front. With so many leaders, we all can't lead at the same time. Put kids first."

I wondered about his comment—"go with less talent and much dedication and purpose"—and the effect it had with teachers. I discussed the point with him later, and he told me that two Highcroft teachers he worked with at his previous school called to say they understood what he meant, but others may have interpreted a lack of emphasis on intellectual development. They encouraged him to put both good persons and cognitive growth on equal footing. He addressed the matter at the February meeting.

In assessing the reactions of teachers, his expectations seemed to be understood. When he drew the line regarding being on time, there was no sign of duress. The "good person" ethic seemed to cover a number of important elements. A good person puts kids first, is on time, and stays beyond the normal contract limits. He charged the group to work hard, a theme from his Depression-era days in Duncans Bridge, when work was valued and expected. He understood that people don't always agree, and while this was normal, they should air their complaints at school rather than the community. Within the first hour of the meeting, Richard covered an enormous set of ideas about educating children and the attributes required for effective teaching. These were punctuated with a summary statement about personal qualities associated with shaping the culture of the school (figure 6).

> Be appreciative, generous, willing. Try hard. Be fun, flexible, well organized. Look good. Be patient, warm, caring, and compassionate. Plan and have the details of the job in hand. Listen to others. Be good housekeepers. Exhibit faith in others. Participate in PTO. Create a warm, inviting teaching and learning environment. Follow a *learning by doing* philosophy. Discuss people and situations in a positive and professional manner. Never use sarcasm. Seldom yell. Look for the good. Follow established procedures. Continue to learn.

All present were attentive, engaged, and perhaps in awe of his rendering of expectations. There was much to assimilate, and no one seemed surprised about the picture Richard painted with his philosophical brush. Everyone present knew him through previous professional connections or others who had worked with him, so his declarations were not new. Teachers wanted to work with Richard and said so during introductions. His reputation for positive leadership, sincere caring for the human side of teaching, and support for teachers was well known. Thus the long march to planning for the opening day began.

Figure 6
Desired Goals for Teachers

- Be appreciative, generous, willing
- Try hard
- Be fun, flexible, & organized
- Exhibit faith in children
- Support the PTO
- Look for the good
- Be patient, caring, & compassionate
- Be ready to teach
- Listen to others
- Follow the "learning by doing" philosophy
- Never use sarcasm, seldom yell
- Be a learning, continue to learn
- Create a welcoming learning environment
- Discuss people and situation in a professional manner
- Look good

Getting Organized

As the meeting continued, task force groups were created for reading, English, science, spelling, maps and globes; and teachers volunteered to serve on each one. Richard outlined an exhaustive list of other task groups as well. These included All Read and All Counsel programs and a plan for activities for the first day of school. Other task force groups included a student helper program, PTO bylaws and constitution, school logo and slogan, a plan for gifted education, computer technology, and a community outreach and volunteer program. It was an immense and daunting list! Perhaps one of the more significant needs mentioned was a method for the care and treatment of each other. He believed teachers were the focal point of everything to be accomplished and that anything worthwhile in a school needs to recognize the work of teachers. Professional teachers are the heart and soul of a school but are often overlooked as change agents. The history of school reform demonstrates that teachers are often looked upon as recipients of change rather than active participants in leading change efforts. A wise principal understood the critical nature of the teacher's role in establishing a positive emotional tone in a school.

Richard also briefly described additional tasks, including selection of audiovisual equipment and material, supply lists, furniture placement, field trip procedures, and the need for representation on district-level curriculum councils in social studies and language arts. Further, each grade-level team was expected to have a teacher help make recommendations on selection of a reading program. Samples of texts from various textbook companies would be available for inspection at the district office in March. Much was expected from the staff over the coming months, and I found myself wondering how it would all come together.

As the formal portion of the meeting approached, copies of the staff roster, calling chain, and the February meeting agenda were provided, and the group shifted to grade-level discussions for the remainder of the session.

Summary

When Richard began teaching at Woodlawn School, he recognized his lack of training and experience. He began to fill the gap through informal and formal training opportunities through the county school district and college extension courses. His introduction to formal study was challenging due to difficulties with reading and comprehension. Through repeated reading of material and sheer determination, he persevered in his studies. One of his professors recognized his difficulty with grammar and punctuation and took extra time to help him diagram sentences.

In order to teach in a country school, organizational skills were critical, and Richard was confident about his ability to pull together the essentials for opening school. Richard believed his experience with organization had its origin in Duncans Bridge and his boyhood experiences in the wheat harvest, working on the farm, and the family grocery store. The capacity for organization was key to success for a country schoolteacher responsible for everything related to school operation. The technical aspects of teaching could be learned day by day, but organization was a foundational skill one had to bring to the job. Figure 4 summarizes important factors brought to the surface during the initial phase of the meeting.

When appointed as principal at Highcroft, Richard developed a written document outlining a sequential plan of action. His penchant for organization was evident in the document that he shared with district-level supervisors. It was titled "Planning for a New School," a dozen or so pages detailing specific tasks, including content for staff meetings that began in January 1978. Broadly speaking, the document contained his institutional plan for Highcroft, and it served as his raison d'être for the new school and himself as leader.

Richard managed the first meeting of the Highcroft staff in a low-key manner, and his relaxed pace helped to moderate the immensity of the agenda. He exhibited an informality that put people at ease in the face of extensive work. His ability to laugh, sometimes at his own foibles, contributed to a positive atmosphere. His manner was instrumental in getting the staff in a groove, a pattern of social interaction fostering team decision-making. Meetings always followed the same process: introductory remarks, overview of the agenda, discussion of identified needs, drawing for door prizes, and grade-level or special area meetings. Through organization, interaction, and pleasant activities, a positive work environment was created and sustained when the school opened in August 1978.

Richard's approach to planning sessions was similar to Abraham Maslow's (1998) theory of motivation based on levels of need. Maslow expressed his vision as a pyramid, where lower-level or basic needs were a starting point. For example, at the bottom of the pyramid, basic physiological needs had to be addressed prior to moving to the next level: safety and security needs. When these needs were satisfied, participants were motivated by social needs, followed by self-esteem, critical thinking, and self-actualization needs. If a lower-level need asserts itself in this progression, progress ceases until immediate needs are addressed.

In an overall sense, Richard's planning sessions mirrored Maslow's approach. Richard was instrumental in creating an environment where basic needs were taken care of. Meetings were well organized. The meeting room was safe and comfortable. The availability of food contributed to sustaining energy after a long day of teaching. Richard presented himself as patient, organized, soft-spoken, and positive. He encouraged a productive social climate conducive to building a team. Without consideration of basic needs, it would have been difficult to engage teachers in complex decisions requiring critical thought. By working through the various levels of human needs, a path to higher order thinking and decision-making was actualized. To make this possible, a leader must be attentive to group processes and demonstrate a readiness to make adjustments when needed. He often made comments like, "We're glad you're here," or "It's good to see you," accompanied by a handshake or hug. The staff responded positively to these expressions.

CHAPTER 5
The Long March to the Opening of School

Important Topics on the February Agenda

The February meeting opened with remarks from the director of research and development. He spoke about his previous experience in helping to start new schools and esprit de corps associated with such a venture. He intended to meet with them prior to the start of school for staff development, and he included himself as one of many in the district office who supported their work. Richard expressed appreciation, and the business of the second meeting began with an invitation to a party for all staff at his home on February 11.

Richard introduced the music teacher and counselor, who were not present in January. His introduction of the school counselor provided details about his training and prior experience, including running in the Boston Marathon. It was clear that Richard planned to call on him for assistance when needed. Richard said that "upon occasion" the counselor would not only assist but, in some circumstances, would "speak for him." He was described as a child-centered counselor and that children would like him, a point confirmed by a staff member whose children were under his guidance at a previous school. For his part, the counselor expressed appreciation to Richard and his excitement as a member of the staff.

School administrators, elementary principals in particular, are middle managers, with teachers and parents on one side and district administrators on the other. It can be a solitary role, or at least feel that way, like a country schoolteacher responsible for everything, and often no one to call on for assistance. Richard often spoke about his burdensome to-do list and his appreciation for help he received from others.

In the interim since the first meeting, teachers had moved quickly on matters of curriculum and instruction. The reading specialist reported that the reading group had met and would meet again in coming weeks. She spoke of her session with book company representatives, indicating that teachers could expect to have feedback during their grade-level meetings. A sixth-grade teacher had been working on science materials, and on one occasion, I observed him eagerly discussing elementary science study (ESS) activities with a group of teachers. He announced that enough ESS materials, sufficient for sixty kids at each grade level, had been ordered and that teachers should make lists of other science materials they wanted. Richard acknowledged his efforts, and he asked the librarian to check with the head of district libraries regarding ESS audiovisual materials and supplementary science materials that could be purchased through the district rather than the school budget.

Another teacher spoke briefly about selection of an English text and samples she had received from book companies. Richard added that primary teachers should feel free to attend her meetings to give input. She welcomed their ideas. The school slogan committee received considerable input from staff members, and several alternatives were presented. The first suggestions included "The very special place," "A great place to grow," "High hopes for Highcroft," and "Growing together." Over the next few months, additional possibilities were brought forward and discussed. Richard told the group they would reach a decision later in the spring.

Physical education teachers talked about their ideas for playground equipment for all age groups. An obstacle course, balance beams, and a tire swing were mentioned, along with their intention to make some of the equipment themselves. They also were in favor of picnic tables near the school, and Richard chimed in, saying, "The children will eat outside the multipurpose room when the weather is good." This was met by approval from everyone.

Reports required more time than expected, and Richard felt the pressure to complete the remainder of the agenda. He moved quickly through updates: including the status of school construction, the ordering of furniture, carpeting, projectors, typewriters, computers, and a host of other material. His secretary managed the paperwork and prepared the purchase orders. He reminded everyone that equipment was intended for use by the entire staff and would be shared, a point originally made at the first meeting. Teachers posed additional questions regarding storage, file cabinets, bulletin boards, and desk arrangements. Richard told his secretary to take notes.

Everyone was curious about the status of school construction. Richard said that weather and shortages of construction materials slowed progress, but the building was under the roof, and he "felt a need to guard it." Teachers wanted to see the inside, and even though far from done, half of them would do so clandestinely in the coming weeks. In his attempt to move things along, Richard recognized that he had "said a lot and probably garbled it up," announcing that he "couldn't keep them late today because his wife expected him home." Additional questions persisted about chalkboards and whiteboards, hooks for maps, dictionaries, and a host of other items, which reflected their interest and enthusiasm for the new facilities. Richard responded patiently, if not completely, to their questions as he ended the meeting.

The pattern of interaction for each meeting was the same, but staff interaction increased as task force groups reported their findings. At the February meeting, a map and globe salesperson discussed materials and responded to many questions from teachers. Following the presentation, Richard talked about grade-level utilization of maps and where they would be located. He also suggested consideration of map materials for first and second grades, asking a teacher to discuss this with the map and globe committee. The decision on map and globes was imminent, and Richard asked, "Are we together on this?" His request for a "yea or nay vote" indicated their agreement.

Task Force Groups—Parent Volunteers

Although meetings started at 4:30 p.m., it was common for individuals to arrive late. Richard never failed to recognize the effort teachers made to attend meetings. Fifteen minutes into the February meeting, a teacher apologized for being late due to makeups for snow days in her district. Richard reacted by saying, "It is OK to be late. I know many of you have come a long way. You look so good after working with kids all day." He was consistent in the way he appreciated both large and small contributions made by teachers. It was apparent that teachers reciprocated with their appreciation of him.

At one point, Richard broached the subject of cursive writing. He said, "When will we introduce cursive writing, in second grade?"

One teacher asked if there was a district policy on this, and Richard responded, "We'll make our own policy." He went on to discuss the Zaner-Bloser program, which he favored, and following a short discussion without dissent, the ZB program was approved.

With each meeting, the opening day of school loomed larger, and there was still much to do. Richard introduced workshop days that were traditional in the opening of school. He said, "We'll have five days for certificated people. How will we spend it?" The question elicited several points of view among teachers. One proposed the workshop be held in the spring. She added that substitute teachers could be hired to free them up, but Richard interjected: "No, if we do that, we'll feel like we are taking you away from your students," not to mention the negative attitudes that other principals would have for such a plan. Others voiced concern about being away from their current students and the extra work required to prepare lessons for the substitute. Following the extended discussion of all sides, Richard stepped in, saying, "I think we have a consensus on five days in August." An additional five days would be devoted to instructional planning prior to opening day. Following an extensive discussion, all approved acceptance of the plan.

Many of the task force groups identified at the January meeting were moving forward. Chief among these was the parent volunteer program. Nearly every aspect of school functioning was to be addressed by a troop of parent volunteers. Three mothers had been identified to head the room mother's program. Three mothers had also accepted responsibility for leading the library assistance group. Another who interestingly did not have children of school age stepped forward to oversee the entire volunteer program. All schools have volunteer programs, but at Highcroft, the extensive involvement of parents was something new in the annals of public education.

Attention was given to the very long list of volunteer programs, and I couldn't help but wonder how all the volunteers would be identified, selected, and trained. The seeds of volunteerism had been planted and nurtured during the spring of 1978 and culminated in an amazing number of community volunteers. Richard was the driving force. His affinity for working with people originated at Duncans Bridge, where everyone was enmeshed in local schools. The concept of school as an extension of the community was evident in Richard's institutional plan.

Following the usual drawing for door prizes and the announcement of the March meeting to be held at Dewey Elementary School to examine library materials, Richard concluded with a few reminders:

1. Make your requisitions legible.
2. If you know good parents that would be good as volunteers, let me know.
3. Be thinking about units you want to teach.
4. Start thinking about field trips during your grade-level meetings,
5. Be thinking about where you want furniture to be placed—everyone gets one move from me." (Additional furniture rearranging would be up to them.)

CHAPTER 6
Building a School Community

Origin of Richard's Ideas about Community

The idea of "community" was deeply rooted in Richard's experience at Duncans Bridge during the Depression, when people had close relationships with family and neighbors. Country schools were established by local farmers, and they organized funding, served on school boards, and took a strong interest in education. Residents saw a direct connection between education and participation in a democratic society. Country schools served as centers for meetings, elections, and social activities, creating a network of support. Having been raised in this atmosphere, the idea of a school community was natural to Richard. As principal, he sought to develop an extensive cadre of volunteers.

As monthly meetings progressed, Richard began a series of informal neighborhood coffees to get acquainted with parents and impart information about plans for the opening of school. As it turned out, twenty-six such gatherings were held between January and June 1978, reaching every neighborhood in the Highcroft attendance area. I attended one of the first coffees in March with Richard, two Highcroft teachers, and eleven mothers.

Richard talked informally with parents as they waited for everyone to arrive. He presented himself in much the same way he did with teachers during planning sessions: soft-spoken, slow cadence, friendly and approachable. He was at ease in such situations, whether with parents or teachers, and if he was the least bit nervous, it was not apparent. He expressed appreciation to the host, smiled often, and was complimentary of questions and comments from mothers. For their part, mothers, mostly in their thirties, were attentive and were not hesitant in asking questions. It was a very informal atmosphere.

Richard introduced himself and the teachers, and he outlined the format for the meeting. "I will go first, and then I want you to talk about your kids, your pet peeves, and what you want the school to be." All present seemed happy with his approach. He began with a recitation of his beliefs about kids and learning:

> Students will learn how to learn and apply what they learn. They will learn how to multiply and divide and understand it. Students will learn how to read and actually do it, enjoy it. They will understand human differences and respect those differences; these kids will not just be an achievement test score. Students will become self-directed people and develop a humane value system: the final test of an education is not just what you know but who you are.

Parents followed his statement of beliefs with interest and smiled with approval. During the 1970s, the discussion of school values was often met with skepticism and outright hostility, but that was not the case with this group of parents. Richard continued with a presentation of five goals, each preceded by either a "try hard" or a promise.

> We will try hard to remember that all children are different, begin where they are, find out what they know first. This is not always an easy thing to do. We will try hard to develop basic skills—responsibutbility, effective work and study habits—but more than just the basics. We promise that Highcroft will be a happy place, having mutual respect. It is a promise that a positive approach will be followed as much as possible, a hugging school. We will try hard to produce fully functioning persons that understand the value of mistakes and have respect for others.

It is worth noting that beliefs and goals he shared with parents were consistent with those discussed with teachers at the first staff meeting, and although not always spoken explicitly, they were evident in the continuing dialogue with parents, teachers, and others in the community. They would eventually form a common language that reached everyone with a stake in the school.

A discussion of how the staff was selected followed. Some were new to the district, some were hired and placed temporarily in other district elementary schools, and some were transferred from within the district. This information was presented in a systematic manner, beginning with the board of education's decision to build the school. He said, "All teachers are a known quantity. There was no pressure to take anyone I didn't want," but he admitted this was a bit scary because he would have to accept responsibility for any poor teachers. He stated that the average age of the teaching staff was between twenty-six and thirty years and all were experienced. For the most part, this was true, but one teacher was new to teaching, having just completed student teaching.

Richard also told the parents about his criteria for hiring teachers. Being a good person was critical, he said, because students often look to teachers as models. His second criterion rested on technical ability; they must have a good grasp of the pedagogy of teaching and learning. Finally, his remarks concluded with a few thoughts to parents: "We need to know when we do good things. We are moving toward a strong volunteer program. We ask every mom and dad to give ten hours of participation to school each year. There will be sixteen different categories for parents to choose from."

On a personal note, he admitted to being defensive at times when he was overtaken by the accumulation of things on his to-do list. He admitted to being human and reassured parents of his intention to try very hard to avoid defensiveness, adding, "We can't always do everything we want to do, but no one will out try us."

Dialogue with Parents

Richard then shifted the meeting to parents and their questions and concerns. In preparation, three guidelines were given. First, they should talk about their children, their ages, and interests. Second, talk about pet peeves but avoid using names of teachers and schools. Third, they were asked to give their ideas about the kind of school they wanted, stated in positive terms. Parents were ready to pose questions.

Parent: "How do you feel about the open classroom?"

Richard: "What is that?"

Parent: "Having a bunch of kids thrown together in an open area."

Richard: "It can be good or bad, depending on such things as the number of students and the teachers involved."

Parent: "I think kids need to be in a more closed setting so they can concentrate better. Will Highcroft be open?"

Richard: "No, but it can be by moving floor to ceiling panels. Kindergarten, first, and second grades will not open their panels. Generally speaking, grades three through six will."

One of the teachers Richard brought to the meeting discussed reasons that second-grade teachers would not open panels except for those times when all four teachers wanted to show a movie or have group reading. Altogether, two other parents raised questions about open space, and another indicated she wasn't concerned because she knew that it was the teacher who made the difference in the classroom. Richard displayed openness in receiving questions about open space. Parents were definitely interested in the subject. An observation made in my field notes during the exchange clarifies the point.

> Richard has handled the questions about open space in an open manner. He intended to show a schematic of the building but didn't get to it. Parents do not seem angry about open space but show real concern. They may have picked up on the controversy that has existed in the school district. Richard and teachers communicate a sense of being in charge of themselves and where they are going. I think parents can easily pick up on this, which should help to allay concern. (Field notes: March 10, 1978)

Richard continued the dialogue with parents.

Parent: "I want Highcroft to be a happy place because happy kids will learn."

Richard: "Bless your heart."

His response was accompanied by a move across the room and a kiss to the woman's head. His action was quite spontaneous and unexpected and produced smiles and giggling from the parents. I believe all the women were impressed by this gesture.

Another parent raised a pet peeve: "I am concerned about language on the bus and fighting or scuffles on the bus and at the bus stop."

One of the teachers responded: "Call us. This is important—just another reason why communication is important. We can often get a hold on these problems early and correct them. Call us anytime you aren't sure."

Another parent: "Can I visit the school?"

Richard: Anytime, but remember we aren't perfect and you may not see us at our best when you come. Keep this in mind and please don't go out and blab it all over the neighborhood. That can be so destructive.

As parent meetings continued, Richard followed the same pattern: welcome and introductions, brief presentation of the planning process, discussion of how parent input would occur, and information about structure of the school building. Extensive open dialogue followed. He maintained his focus on listening and being open to all questions, even uncomfortable ones, such as open space. Figure 7 summarizes steps in developing community outreach.

The teachers who attended were important in answering questions and expanding upon various points made by Richard. There was familiarity in the way Richard and teachers conducted themselves. Teachers smiled often, appeared friendly, and were positive. Richard and teachers were interested in the same questions and concerns held by parents. He talked easily about the selection criteria for staff members. He wanted teachers who were good persons, for children tend to model the behavior of teachers. Richard sought technically competent teachers who could work collaboratively.

Throughout the long series of parent coffees, the only serious concern revolved around open space, yet parents seemed to accept Richard's flexible stance, at least for the moment, regarding the ability to open room dividers within a pod. The meetings conveyed Richard's confidence in teachers who would be responsible for determining how flexible space would be used in support of learning.

**Figure 7
Building a School Community**

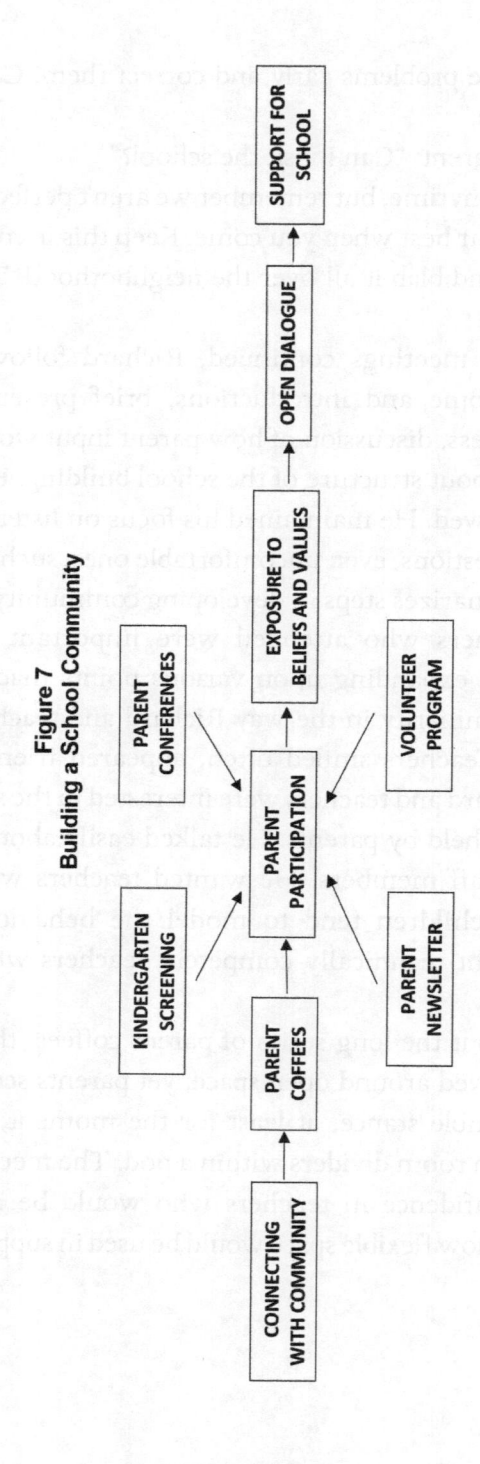

```
                          SUPPORT FOR
                             SCHOOL
                               ↑
                         OPEN DIALOGUE
                               ↑
                         EXPOSURE TO
                      BELIEFS AND VALUES
                               ↑
     PARENT                                VOLUNTEER
   CONFERENCES                              PROGRAM
        ↘                                     ↙
                         PARENT
                      PARTICIPATION
        ↗                   ↑                 ↖
   KINDERGARTEN                            PARENT
    SCREENING                            NEWSLETTER
                               ↑
                          PARENT
                          COFFEES
                               ↑
                       CONNECTING
                     WITH COMMUNITY
```

56   G. Wayne Mosher

CHAPTER 7
Substantive Additions to the Planning Schedule

Looking Ahead

In March, Richard presented the staff with a list of remaining planning sessions, including changes in the meeting schedule, additional meetings with grade-level teams, and special area groups to discuss substantive issues. For example, the length of the lunch period and how it was to be supervised was something Richard wanted the entire staff to consider. The school schedule and matters of supervision required study, discussion, and approval. Another example that figured prominently in the daily lives of teachers was school discipline and procedures. Other matters of less strategic importance included the amount of time and kinds of materials devoted to the use of television within classrooms and the need for an articulation plan to facilitate a smooth transition between grade levels and middle school.

There was always much to be done, and the vast majority of it could have been accomplished solely, and possibly more expeditiously, by one person, the principal. When he set forth his idea of staff as an empowered community working together in making decisions, he knew that a slower deliberative approach was required. This position was captured in the wisdom of a well-known African proverb: "If you want to go quickly, go alone, but if you want to go far, go together." Richard clearly wanted "to go far."

Within the evolving and crowded agenda, Richard regularly reviewed progress and often added additional task force and study groups to his existing list. By March 1978, eighteen task force groups were formed, each staffed by a complement of teachers and paraprofessionals. In addition, a significant number of study groups formed earlier continued to work on a variety of subjects. With three months of planning meetings remaining and a five-day training workshop prior to the opening of school, the tension was palpable. In the face of this reality, the staff shouldered the schedule and timeline with good humor.

Important Elements in the Final Months of Planning

Late in March, Richard convened a session to examine library materials. It was held at the librarian's school, where an extensive collection of books, supplementary items, and audiovisual resources were made available for informal examination by Highcroft teachers. This coincided with preparation of purchase orders for the Highcroft LRC. With food and coffee in hand, teachers examined everything with great interest.

Richard opened the formal meeting with a request for feedback about the parent meetings that several teachers had attended. A variety of observations were shared. One teacher said the meetings projected good feelings" and that "open-space questions were handled well. They will see that we are well organized."

For the benefit of all teachers who had not yet attended a coffee, a teacher described the specifics of Richard's agenda from beginning to end. A fourth-grade teacher stated, "Parents enjoyed talking with teachers in a relaxed atmosphere." The coffees helped parents become acquainted with each other and teachers, helping to create a connection with the community.

As the parent coffees continued, concerns about open space diminished and were replaced by other ideas identified by parents. Only one of the twenty-six meetings produced any serious questions about open space. Parents were more interested in school start and end times, kindergarten registration, and whether their child would attend morning or afternoon sessions. Questions parents may have had about teachers were preempted by the information Richard dispensed about the staff and school building. He alluded to a construction report given to the board of education March 21 that indicated "good progress after a slow start due to bad weather." Later the board approved the start time of 8:40 a.m. and end time of 3:10 p.m. for Highcroft.

I met briefly with Richard on March 22 as a follow-up to the most recent planning session. By this time, most of the staff was in regular attendance, with the exception of two third-grade teachers with schedule conflicts and graduate studies. After discussions with the absent teachers, they agreed not to continue and were eventually replaced. This was the only glitch in Richard's careful staff selection process.

As the end of the 1977–1978 school year neared, the planning sessions began to wind down. The May meeting addressed initiatives begun earlier in the year, and progress reports were given by teachers who continued to complete their work. A significant amount of time was given to the reading program, its organization, and materials. Reading is one of the significant components in the elementary school curriculum because of its ramifications for other curriculum areas. The reading specialist had been working diligently over the last several months, and the time had come to engage the faculty in the manner it would be implemented. It was a total school program, cutting across all grade levels, affecting everyone in the school through its companion structure, the All Read Program. In addition, ordering of materials for language arts and social studies also needed to be completed. In addition, the long-awaited decision on school logo and slogan awaited final agreement.

Richard opened the May 2 meeting with introductions of three room mothers. He knew these women through parent coffees, and they seemed comfortable with his sense of humor and positive style. Each gave the assembled staff a few words of introduction, followed by a brief discussion regarding their intentions. Becoming better acquainted with grade-level interests and needs would be the chief guiding factor in their service. They were well received. The exchange between the women, Richard, and staff was warm and pleasant. Teachers were clearly interested in volunteers and welcomed them to the school community. Richard summarized the segment by saying, "The key thing is that they want to serve—not just parties but in other ways."

One of the teachers reported on the need to select a spelling program. She was part of the district level committee charged with making recommendations. The field of choices had been reduced to three: Kottmeyer, phonetic approach, and Lippincott. She indicated that no one on the committee was excited about the choices. Richard asked for suggestions on how to proceed. The teacher suggested that each grade level identify a person to send their recommendation to her. Another teacher suggested that it might be appropriate to first clarify why they wanted students to spell—for vocabulary, or writing, or both—as a basis for selection. Richard then confirmed the suggestion that each grade level identify a representative to give their preference.

The Prominence of the Reading Curriculum

The weighty issue of reading continued as Richard turned to his reading specialist to take the lead. The program was initiated several months ago, when each school selected a representative to the district reading committee. In the interim, the committee selected the program from Houghton Mifflin, and the reading specialist provided a sheet outlining the rationale for the decision. She began: "There is a need for teams to get together and list in prioritized order the Houghton Mifflin supplementary materials [readers, workbooks, and so forth] that they want." She provided everyone with a paper describing the strengths of the program, including the sequential approach that builds reading skills. It outlined specific assists such as phonic cues, sight words, and natural speech patterns that were reinforced throughout the levels. According to her experience, the program was research based and fostered a love of reading. It was a compelling list of strengths.

Earlier in the narrative, I discussed the fact that most teachers selected for Highcroft had teaching experience in schools with self-contained classrooms. In nearly all cases, reading was a district program that everyone was expected to follow. However, in the isolation of the self-contained classroom, teachers often used materials they liked and had experience with and used in conjunction with the district program. However, a different set of expectations existed at Highcroft, where team decision-making was expected. Within this reality, there was a potential for conflict. Would teachers be willing to give up the tendency to use their favorite materials even though they may not align with the reading program? This pitfall could be minimized by the reading specialist's suggestion for teams to compile lists of supplementary materials to accompany Houghton Mifflin. I wondered what would happen when actual implementation occurred. Would everyone adhere to the alternatives they proposed to the reading specialist? Or would teachers still be compelled to use their old tried-and-true materials? The validity of the Houghton Mifflin program would depend on the degree of collaboration within each team.

The reading specialist continued. "Does anyone have difficulty with grouping kids for reading? It's important that if anyone does have difficulty with this, now is the time to discuss it." There was no response from the group. She followed up: "Students will read in their own classrooms, whether they are low or high; they will not be sent out." This points to the significance of grade-level teachers selecting good supplementary materials. She also asked them to consider extra readers from a different series, SRA kits, and other materials that build skills. Within the existing environment of high stakes testing at several levels, an atmosphere of accountability exists within the core programs of schools. This tends to heighten the importance of consistent implementation of the curriculum in order to achieve the desired level of pupil performance indicated by in-house research conducted by Houghton Mifflin. Teachers were aware of accountability in their professional work, and heightened awareness creates tension. At Highcroft, as well as other schools where team decision-making is practiced, the connection between curriculum and instructional methods is prominent. One could expect to see high achievement. All matters of curriculum integrity were influenced by the degree of compliance from team decision-making.

Richard summarized the exchange between the reading specialist and staff. He spoke briefly about the preparation of requisitions and then asked the reading specialist to talk about her role. "There is no way I can service all the kids. You will need to help me set priorities. Do we hit kindergarten and primary or upper grades? These are tough tradeoffs, and I hope our parent volunteers can help us." She added that she was going to train some parent volunteers with the kinds of help skills that could assist teachers in helping students.

Richard was following the discussion closely. He indicated that he and his guidance counselor would soon be going to elementary schools where prospective Highcroft kids were located, to begin looking for students who had problems, including reading. He quickly followed with a request for the reading specialist to continue discussing her plan of attack.

"Houghton Mifflin says start them at grade level. Identify them as soon as possible. There should be no testing early in the year because of confusion [during the opening of school] Around the third week, use placement tests to help form reading groups." Richard clarified: "We won't try to do anything with reading the first three weeks. We'll want to get to know them and have them feel good about us."

The All Read Program was a favorite of Richard's because it promoted reading for pleasure while reinforcing reading skills. At a prescribed time one day each week, normal activities would cease and everyone—children, secretaries, paraprofessionals, custodians, and so on—would stop and read a book. Students were to be encouraged to bring favorite books from home. It was unusual to be in a school that was completely quiet. The reading specialist suggested teachers arrange to have books from the library available. The librarian quickly added that the library should be ready but perhaps not as "established" as their old schools. She asked the reading specialist to keep this in mind. One of the physical education teachers informed the group that all special area teachers would be scheduled into grade levels to assist teachers during the All Read time.

Throughout the discussion about details of the reading program, teachers were tuned in and listening. Reading was pivotal to successful achievement. The implementation of the reading program had its own specialness because it differed in the way it was implemented in other elementary schools. The reading specialist said, "We are unique in the district in that we have a commitment to individualizing reading. This is really neat, and I appreciate everyone's efforts. Other schools have talked about doing it but never did." The moment was memorialized in my field notes: "Observation. This could be a unifying theme for the Highcroft staff, an innovation that sets them apart from other schools in district."

As the meeting moved closer to adjournment, Richard called attention to several brief reports about remaining tasks. One of the physical education teachers provided information on the school schedule that she and three other teachers were preparing. At the time, this struck me as somewhat unusual. The schedule is almost a sacred entity to a school. It specifies teacher team planning time, lunch periods, and the movement of students to special programs like art, music, and physical education, including when they are delivered and picked up by their regular teacher. It becomes the framework within which everything is accomplished. It requires submission by all who are governed by it. More often than not, the principal would assume the task and accept the consequences for implementation. Richard wanted teachers involved because they would be more likely to accept and respect it.

In her brief report, she said that the best thing about planning the schedule so far was forty minutes for team planning each day. She also stated that each teacher would have a thirty-five-minute lunch period without responsibility for supervising student lunchtimes. Her report was met with murmurs of approval from the group. She said the schedule committee would continue to formalize the plan, and Richard would have responsibility for managing it. For instance, given that teachers would have a duty-free lunch period, how would lunch periods be supervised? A complicating matter was the commitment Richard made to the physical education team, who wanted to use the multipurpose area for PE during the lunchtime, which in turn created an additional question about where students ate lunch. In his efforts to involve teachers in key aspects of planning, Richard unveiled two potent problems requiring creative solutions. He pondered these problems for some time before revealing solutions just prior to the opening of school.

The art teacher reported on books, art prints, and inexpensive paperback books for the art room. She spoke of her need to talk with grade-level teams to demonstrate how parent volunteers would assist in the art studio. The school nurse described her meeting with mothers who volunteered in the nurse's office. She was followed by the counselor's discussion of kindergarten screening to be held May 22 and the need for assistance from teachers. He laughed as he said, "Richard has volunteered some of you to help with the screening." Teachers accepted his tongue-in-cheek remark, and several volunteered for the six screening sessions he scheduled.

He went on to tell the staff that several parents had made specific requests to place children with certain teachers who were rejected out of hand because they were unfair and created negative sentiments in the school and community. He said, "Kids are going to see a variety of teachers," implying that learning to work with a variety of people is important to good citizenship. "If any parent asks you about this [requests for a teacher], refer them to Richard." Considerable laughter followed. Richard smiled.

The meeting ended amid a flurry of questions. Richard tried to engage them in a list of remaining stuff they still needed to do. "Look at your handout. It will be our work list. We don't need to feel that it all should get done right away." The librarian joked about his spelling of the word *group* (*gruop*) on the handout. Earlier Richard had jokingly criticized her handwriting. Good-natured satire was a characteristic of the dialogue in these meetings.

Richard's secretary discussed duplicating procedures. Another teacher wondered aloud if everything had been ordered. A sixth-grade teacher wanted to know where the telephones would be located. Richard responded to all questions, including one about the intercom system in the building.

Richard: "The intercom system is very modern."

Secretary: "Yes, it has a cassette deck for all his country music." (Much laughter.)

Richard: "Yes, and I can listen in on teacher's classrooms, and [smiling] I will." (Followed by delayed but hearty laughter.)

The evening ended with a brief presentation by a teacher from the district math project who spoke about math manipulatives available through the project. Richard asked teachers to pay close attention to materials that could be paid for by math project funds, thus saving building funds for other needs. It was 6:25 p.m., and several teachers began to leave.

The final planning session was held May 31 and continued to address many loose ends. During the month, Richard and the school counselor met with students who would attend Highcroft in the fall. Kids had the typical questions: "Can we ride our bikes to school?" "What will we do in science?" "How often will we have gym?" "Will we change classes?" "When will school start?"

Richard tried to respond to the flurry of questions, but there were too many to deal with, so he said, "If there is something you want to ask me about that you couldn't say, then call me. I'm in the book. If I'm not home, my wife will take a message." Excited smiles were abundant, which brought forth positive comments from Richard: "We know we're going to have a very good school. You are good kids." Richard told them they could continue to think of themselves as students in their current school until school was out, "when you will become Highcroft kids." He urged them to not brag about it because it could cause hurt feelings among other students.

Richard and the counselor also met with principals and counselors from "feeder" schools to develop insights about students with unique or special needs. These meetings helped identify those who might need a pat on the back from Richard. The counselor followed up with information to be shared with teachers.

The band and strings teachers were introduced, along with the replacements for two third-grade teachers who had scheduling conflicts, preventing attendance at meetings. These additions brought the team to full strength. The reading specialist and other teachers chairing task groups reported on reading materials that had been ordered, possible English text options, and the spelling program that Richard took time to highlight. "Do you understand what she is saying about spelling? We are using Heath, when the rest of the district wanted something else. It means we have to be ready with our explanation. You will have to pre-post test [a means to determine skills before and after introduction of units] to use Heath." Varying from district level programs is a risk when local curriculum choices cause unwanted questions from district program coordinators.

Richard was pleased with the response he received from parents who wanted to be school volunteers. The counselor discussed volunteers who assisted with kindergarten screening, stating, "They worked hard all day. They were stretched out, tired. It helped them understand how it is for teachers." Richard added, "Mothers saw how we worked with kids with a good bit of stress." Allowing parents to participate and observe teachers in action underlined his sense of transparency.

The issue of the school slogan and logo came up, and Richard asked teachers to look over the examples in the handout his secretary provided. He stated, "We need to have something that can be picked up and said easily." Richard believed an emblem or verse that embodied quality was important, and to that end, he suggested an idea similar to the Nabisco product label because it was well known and recognized as a great product. The idea was not well received and led to alternatives such as soliciting ideas from parents or having a contest where students could contribute ideas. The staff liked this idea, but with the start of school looming large, and the need to create a handbook and documents for parents, Richard wondered about the time required. The staff was continuing to examine alternatives when Richard interjected: "Are we saying we don't have something that strikes us yet?" Teachers responded that they were. Sensing the importance of the matter, a teacher recommended "Highcroft Ridge, a great place to grow," adding that children could then decide on the logo. So the cover for the school handbook and other documents showed a drawing of three children, books in hand and smiling, on their way to school. Although it would have several revisions over the years, that was the choice for the moment. Time had run out. Vacations were planned, and everyone needed a respite from the intensity of the last several months.

In June, following the planning sessions, I talked with Richard about the several months of planning. He stated that the primary goal was to build relationships and trust within the staff. A closely related goal was reaching a consensus about a sense of direction for the school. He was aware of the mountain of work to be accomplished and believed the time spent would be critical to a successful opening. He thought the planning sessions helped to establish cooperative decision-making and his commitment to a democratic approach to school leadership.

The majority of teachers spoke positively about planning meetings, although some complained about the long days after being in a classroom all day. For the most part, teachers believed they got to know each other personally, learned about each others' strengths and shortcomings, and taken together, initially helped to promote good working relationships.

Starting a new school from scratch was Richard's dream. For him, the stakes were high. The teachers who had worked with him previously could sense when he was having a bad day. He set his goals so high that when something went wrong, it affected him. However, they admired Richard for his positive, personable style and commented that he "builds up people, believes you will succeed, and brings out the very best in people." One teacher said, "Richard is the most influential person in my life outside my family. He was a constant in my life."

Amid the accolades, teachers were aware that he was not perfect. "If someone is really great, they are going to make enemies. Richard can put it on the line when necessary, and sometimes it's hard for people to take that. Not everyone is going to say that he walks on water." Richard was aware of his strengths and weaknesses, which some principals try to hide. When seeking to be a good person, which I believe Richard strived to be, his positive and not-so-positive aspects were visible for all to see.

Richard was confident about his work. The ambition and determination that marked his earlier life accompanied him through the years. At Highcroft, success, at least in part, rested on his selection of teachers, a process that he generally felt good about. The selection of one teacher at each grade level with prior work experience with Richard was strategic. Even though it wasn't openly discussed, it was implicit that those teachers, all with several years of experience, would be leaders in the implementation of plans.

Richard recognized his need for control, but experience had taught an important lesson about empowerment. Although the public may see schooling as a simple, straightforward process, the reality is that teaching and learning are quite complex and leadership of schools is equally complex. At a basic level, whether a school is successful or not depends on the degree of ownership that teachers have in the process. Richard's approach to empowering teachers and parents as participants in a school community suggests a keen mind and determination to achieve desired outcomes. In many ways, he was fortunate to have grown up in a small rural town during the Depression, where he learned to value the interdependence that binds a community together.

CHAPTER 8
Highcroft Ridge Elementary School Takes Flight

Orientation

On Monday August 21, 1978, five days of pre-school meetings began at Highcroft as workers attempted to complete a host of unfinished tasks. As I looked around the group of teachers and staff, everyone appeared rested and ready to get started. Richard looked tanned and relaxed as he launched the meeting with introductions of two new staff members. He spoke about construction difficulties: carpeting not installed, undelivered cabinets and furniture, and uncertain delivery of school supplies and equipment. Richard said, "I hope we can concentrate on what we have rather than on what we don't have. I've learned that contractors view school jobs as 'milk runs': they are very slow."

The agenda for the day was full. Two assistant superintendents were scheduled to speak later in the morning, so Richard began with matters of immediate need. Attention was called to a large notepad at the edge of the library, where teachers could list needs and concerns for later consideration. Bus behavior was briefly discussed. He talked about emergency plans, office duplication procedures, and where they could find construction paper ("in a silo next to third grade"). One of the teachers asked him what a silo was, and he said, "OK, for all of you who are as dumb as Diane ..." He explained that it was a storage area and told them where it was located. As in the past, exchanges like these were taken with good humor and everyone laughed, including the teacher who'd posed the question.

Richard gave a brief history of Highcroft, beginning with board of education approval in 1975. A detailed review of the staff selection process was given, followed by an outline of his expectations. "I want to emphasize that each of you is Highcroft School," a point that carried important significance. Teachers and staff were seen as representatives of not just the "place" but people that had a stake in school success. It suggested that they represented not just themselves but also the core values and beliefs about the education of children. They were not just mere participants but people who helped to shape the school as an organization.

Richard continued:

> There are great expectations in the community, also from me and the board of education. I know it will be a good school, a kid-centered school. I know much emphasis will be placed on kids' self-image. This business [education] is imprecise, but I am sure of one thing: building the child's self-image.

He spoke of a certain truth regarding the opening of school:

> The first few weeks will determine how the year goes. It's going to be hard work in view of carpeting not completely done and much cabinetry and desks

not here yet. Clerical supplies and typewriters aren't ready either. I hope we can concentrate on what we have rather than on what we don't have.

Richard, forever the optimist, tried to put a good face on a problem that could not be immediately solved.

The anticipated opening of school was significant in the minds of everyone present and heightened by brief presentations from two representatives from the district office. The assistant superintendent for elementary education discussed the origin of the school, beginning with the board of education mandate in 1975. He estimated 775 pupils during the first year, which led to a friendly exchange with Richard, who predicted an enrollment closer to 800.

The assistant superintendent for curriculum and instruction spoke at length about community expectations. He said, "For the most part, the community does not want to see any change in good teaching practices, but they tack on a 'however': give good counseling to children, avoid accidents on the playground, show parents the test scores, and meet with parents to allay concerns." His remarks provoked a few questions from teachers:

Teacher: "What do we do?"

Assistant superintendent: "Remember that they [parents] come from some anxiety, real or imagined. They are concerned about the drug problems in junior high."

Richard: "What forces are working out there in the community?"

Assistant superintendent:

> A small group of people who are almost totally disenchanted with public schools and what their kids experienced. Their response is withdrawal! They are disenchanted with the reading program and enrichment. This group would probably be happy if you brought out the nineteen forty syllabus, which

taught language arts, physical education, science, and math. In this atmosphere, I don't think we could pass a [tax] levy.

Richard: "What advice would you give us as we plan?"
Assistant superintendent:

Think of all the things that parents need to know so they won't be surprised. You are building a reputation, and it's a fragile thing. Give them a sequential picture of what you are going to do. You don't have to do this every year. Tell them about skills and how you are going to help build self-image. Also, talk about remedial education.

His words exposed a reality that all schools were faced with in the late twentieth century. He explained that most parents probably didn't understand the complexities involved in teaching children. Substance abuse, a focus on performance testing, legislative involvement in the control of funding, and academic content was not as pronounced during the period they attended school. He suggested several concerns to keep in mind: "Sixty-two percent of parents want information about schools. Give information in several ways. What is being taught, how is my child doing, what are the rules? Public confidence in institutions is slipping. It is a general indictment that hits schools too."

If his remarks did nothing else, they underscored the critical nature of communicating with parents and significant people in the community, which coincided with Richard's thoughts about closing the gap between school and home. The development of an extensive volunteer program, careful attention to appropriate written and verbal communications, support of an enthusiastic parent-teacher organization, and the alignment of procedures with district-level patterns for relating to the public demonstrated the high level of attention Richard gave to community outreach.

Public Relations

Later in the week, Richard asked the district director of public relations to share her perspective on reaching out to the public. He introduced her: "This is Carol Green. She's a good friend, and she's been with us for a long time."

Her tenure in the district was obvious in the way she presented the history of the school district, the expansion of enrollments over the years, and the need to bring residents together in support of schools and school bond elections. The need to earn public respect was paramount to the board of education and superintendent, and everyone in the district had a role to play. She said, "We want to earn public support. Hold on to it because it can be easily lost through misunderstandings." Her presentation included examples of effective communication tools and ways to build bridges both ways.

Carol offered four goals that formed the foundation for school-home relations: "Maintain good internal relationships. Try to solve problems in- house."

Richard added, "We call that our keep your mouth shut policy."

Carol continued: "Integrity, competency, and hard work. There is no substitute for it." She emphasized that teachers needed to draw from a repertoire of effective techniques and share their knowledge and skill with parents. She urged teachers to prepare written communications that were grammatically correct and "letter perfect." She underscored the importance of sharing essential information such as bus and lunch schedules, emergency plans, and procedures for bad weather and school closings. And above all else, "help to protect the reputation of the school district." Teachers were attentive. Many took notes and posed several questions. When I interviewed Carol several days later regarding her presentation, she stated that Richard's work with the Highcroft staff was unparalleled in the school district with regard to public relations. She said that much of what she shared was already in progress at Highcroft.

Originally, Richard had set aside two weeks for pre-school meetings. Along the way, he scaled it down to five days, which allowed the remaining five days for team meetings and teacher work time in preparation for the first day. The time was welcomed by everyone and was interrupted only for the school dedication program on August 30.

When the staff meeting reconvened after lunch, Richard continued discussion of immediate needs and concerns related to the opening of school. One concern was making sure children could find the correct bus at the end of the day. Earlier a third-grade teacher proposed some sort of card system to guide students to the correct bus. Richard asked the teacher to work up something they could consider. He said, "Are we together enough on the procedures for opening school?" Silence appeared to indicate approval. He thanked everyone for turning off the lights when they left their work area and followed with another reminder: "Don't put the word *require* next to things you want the children to bring to school. Failure to do so would put the school in conflict with the attorney general's ruling regarding items the school should supply. We'll have to find a way of getting around this ruling.

"Now, you're not going to take stuff that belongs to colleagues, are you?" While not a significant problem, teachers are adept at gathering materials from a variety of sources. Richard followed with, "Who took the math stuff off the cart in the fourth grade? The one with the note around the cart [saying *don't take*]." His remark was received with a bit of laughter and some knowing smiles, and Richard didn't push it further. Message sent!

Richard continued:

> There are three words I should never use: *never, forever,* and *ever.* But will you please never get into

the duplicating equipment? It means that if you are thinking about something you need while at breakfast, it will not get done when you need it. We need two days of advance notice. We will try to take care of emergencies too.

This segment of the meeting also addressed a litany of dos and don'ts for teachers to follow:

Never put a kid in the hall for punishment. Children should not have to copy pages from a dictionary. No punishments where a child has to write 'I will not do [something] a hundred times'. A child should not miss lunch. A child should not miss music, art, and physical education as punishments for misbehavior. Don't give sweets as a reward but occasionally as a special treat. Move children quietly along corridors. There will be a few hard heads [children] who won't go along and will need some logical consequences and talk in order to reach them. Our discipline will be so good that it will influence behavior at the mall.

Addressing Last-Minute Issues

The parent volunteer program was evolving nicely behind the scenes. Richard told the group that the first edition of the parent newsletter would be sent to each household before the opening of school. It provided a means for sustaining parent communications about important information such as lunch schedules, emergency procedures, and upcoming events. Three mothers chaired the newsletter group. They were among several hundred parents involved in a wide range of volunteerism at the school.

Richard drew attention to a group of men from a shelter in the inner city whom he'd hired to help get school organized for the first day. He asked the staff to thank them for their work, stating, "Help the men from the city feel welcome and appreciated. Tell them thanks for helping. It's an example of what can be done if people invest in other people."

His recitation eventually gave way to spontaneous questions of teachers on a variety of items not previously discussed:

Teacher: "Do students stay after school or not?"

Richard: "As far as I'm concerned, no. But if you think it's needed and you inform parents, then OK. On the positive, yes, if you contact parents."

Fourth-grade teacher: "Could we have a policy on parties? What if a student comes to one of us and wants a surprise party for another teacher?"

There was a brief silence before Richard responded.

Richard: "I always like the way fourth-grade teachers lead us into these things. I can go either way. What do you want to do?"

There was some brief discussion about parties, and Richard responded with a caveat: "The suggestion seems to be that if you do choose to have a party, be sure to involve room mothers. I'll make a note on this, and we'll discuss it later."

Librarian: "I would like the science film loops returned to the library to be put on cards. I think they are best stored there."

She spoke rather authoritatively, which generated a rebuttal from a fourth-grade teacher. However, the librarian logically pointed out that since teachers would have to check out a projector anyway, they would have convenient access to the visual material. Richard supported the librarian's logic, saying, "I don't think anyone will lose them."

Teacher: "What is your policy on student use of telephones?"

Richard: "There are many things that teaching teams will have to decide on, but I think you probably won't want kids to use phones in the class areas." Teachers accepted his point of view and murmured agreement among themselves.

One might think that operational details such as these would have been addressed prior to the week before school opened.

Again, the enormity of details to be considered, beginning from zero, at least in part, explained last-minute considerations. Even in established schools, it is not uncommon for the school year to begin with unresolved issues.

As break time approached, Richard spoke with sensitivity about things that seemed most important to their plans for opening day. He said, "Relax and enjoy the opening of school. Get acquainted with kids, build rapport, have fun. Keep busy work to a minimum. Think about student needs. End each day with an assessment of what has been accomplished." Lastly was some advice that all accepted with humor: "Don't you dare bitch, moan, or cry at me about something you don't have. I've moved every damn thing in this building three times." He followed this with an expectation he'd recited many times since January 23, when planning meetings began: Don't bad-mouth this school or your colleagues," an iteration of his mantra regarding solving problems at school and not in the neighborhood.

CHAPTER 9
The First Day of School

Organized and Prepared

In early August, Richard sent a letter to children and parents about the opening of school: arrival and departure times, bus transportation, bicycles, medications, and other details. It began with a list of some of the goals for the school year, and the first one was prominent: be a good person. Richard believed that sound human qualities formed the foundation of a good school. Everything else followed from this belief. The twelve goals outlined in his letter were those communicated to teachers and parents earlier in the year.

The letter urged parents to continue to work with their children on common courtesy: using good judgment with hands, feet, and mouth and emphasizing good behavior at the bus stop and on the bus. The letter concluded with, "Continue to help your child to be a good person."

August 31, 1978, was a momentous day and the culmination of months of preparation. Like the launching of a ship, Highcroft Ridge was about to have its own version of a shake down cruise. Given the usual issues of overloaded and late buses, children who weren't picked up, preparation of revised bus schedules, and last-minute scurrying of construction workers trying to complete tasks, everyone was ready for the anticipated seven-hundred-plus children. Richard and teachers were welcoming students outside the front door. Secretaries were busy preparing new bus cards for students and announcements about changes in bus routes to be sent home to parents. As usual, the office staff responded to these unanticipated needs with a degree of frustration as they soldiered on with a smile. Such is the life of school secretaries, often inundated with problems demanding immediate attention.

Lunch Procedures

The success of any school day, at least in part, may be judged by the orderliness of the lunch procedure. Under normal circumstances, children eat in the cafeteria, but at Highcroft, lunch was served in the multipurpose area, which presented two problems. First, in order to serve seven-hundred-plus children, there was no time for a leisurely lunch. Students arrived in shifts from classrooms, obtained their food, ate with a degree of urgency, and returned to class areas. A second issue was the desire of the PE teachers to access the multipurpose area for activities during lunchtime, when the gym was in use. In order to cope with these issues, Richard developed a plan whereby teachers would take children to get lunches that were then taken back to project areas to eat. Since teachers were allowed a duty-free lunch period, Richard had arranged for custodians, office aides, and himself to supervise. This arrangement would prove to be a challenge in terms of logistics, cleanup, and behavior management, requiring several weeks to address.

The school building was as ready as it could be given delays in essential equipment and supplies. To be accurate, the school was beautiful. Walls were painted with warm hues, with matching carpet colors throughout. Thanks to Richard's wife, Myra, every classroom had a rocking chair she had painted. She also arranged tables with lamps at various hallway locations to soften the glare of florescent lights. Antiques and artwork depicting early American themes were found at every turn. Taken together, all these accents helped create a homelike atmosphere, a comfortable place for teaching and learning. These attributes were also visible in the Overfelt residence and likely influenced by country values around Duncans Bridge many years earlier.

A Successful First Day

As the day progressed, teachers were busy introducing school procedures and working with children on activities. The sound emanating from these open spaces was moderate and did not appear to cause distraction. Overall, teachers had prepared well for the first day, and everyone was engaged. As the end of the day approached, teachers were observed helping children complete their work, and some were reading quietly to students. Everything, except lunchtime, moved smoothly. The custodians assigned to project areas where students ate were doing so without the assistance of the clerical aides, as they were busy in the office. One of them said it was "disorganized and hectic," and another found it hard to supervise and pick up trash at the same time. However, another custodian took a broader view, stating, "It was the first time getting used to eating in project areas. It will get better as time goes on."

Overall, Richard was pleased with the day. However, bus transportation was an issue. Unlike established schools with well-defined bus routes and knowledgeable drivers, Highcroft lacked this history; the entire enterprise had to be learned. Richard noted, "One group of thirty children was passed by a driver, and another wound up with one hundred kids to pick up." On the surface, it didn't seem to be a huge problem—unless one was on the office staff, which had to prepare new bus routes, bus IDs, and information for parents. In this one respect, the stress of the first day was acutely felt. However, when the parent-produced newsletter, *The Highcroft Ridge Hotline Reporter*, was published, one of the articles addressed the opening:

> Thursday morning, August 31, 1978, brought the opening of district schools, and for those of us at Highcroft Ridge, administration, teachers, office and volunteer workers, parents, and especially the children, it was a day full of excitement, apprehension, work, and fun. Everything seemed to go very smoothly. Our impressions of the school are that it provides an atmosphere conducive to good learning and happy, cheerful productive and responsible children. (Highcroft Ridge Hotline Newletter, volume 1, September 1978)

CHAPTER 10
Teaching in an Open-Plan School

First Encounters with Flexible Space

During the initial planning stages, the question of open space and how it would ultimately be used was on the minds of teachers and parents. It is important to remember that teachers selected by Richard for Highcroft had no previous experience with open-space arrangements. Some parents had direct knowledge through exposure in other school districts throughout the country, and others heard negative comments from parents within the school district. The subject was brought up at some of the coffees Richard held, and parents were cautious or genuinely concerned in their views about how it would work at Highcroft. Richard took the position that the utilization of space is a choice that rests with teaching teams at each grade level. His premise was that opening the flexible walls within a grade-level pod would be an advantage when a large group activity was planned. At other times, teams might close the flexible walls as they worked with smaller groups. He communicated the idea of "flexible space utilization" whenever the subject came up.

Whether a school is open or more traditional, classroom

instruction ultimately depends upon the training and effectiveness of teachers. Richard hired teachers he believed were instructionally sound and excellent in relating to children. He wanted good persons first, and second, technical excellence in teaching. Richard had never led a completely open-space school, but in a previous school district, he'd chaired a committee of principals and teachers in designing a school with flexible space and alternative teaching methods. A plan was produced and set to be implemented when Richard accepted a position in the Parkway School District. Alternative methods of teaching and learning had been percolating in his thoughts and actions for some time. He was prepared to plan such a school if the opportunity presented itself, as it did at Highcroft. Thus I sought to understand the way teaching teams planned and implemented instructional activities within the open-space setting. After school began, when teachers had settled into their routines, I began to observe teachers at work and more generally throughout the school. My own background as a member of a science team in an open-space high school sharpened the focus of my observations.

During a visit on September 5, I watched a first-grade teacher engage children in a charade game. The children were seated on the carpet as the teacher discussed procedures. She told the children to think of a particular activity or setting as she moved among them, listening to their whispered ideas. The children were enthusiastic, and the teacher was positive, accepting all their suggestions. She then pantomimed their ideas as they tried to guess the meaning. Children were wide-eyed, smiling, and excited as the activity unfolded. The underlying aim was enhancement of thinking skills and creativity. A bit later, in a similar vein, a third-grade teacher arranged students in groups to pantomime a scheme as the other children hypothesized the underlying theme of group presentations.

Two fifth-grade teachers opened the flexible wall between their classrooms to teach a math lesson using Popsicle sticks, demonstrated by a member of the district math project. Upon hearing about the lesson, two fourth-grade teachers quickly involved the project leader in the same lesson, opening the flexible wall between their classrooms to facilitate a large group event. Flexibility with regard to the use of space was especially advantageous when unanticipated resources became available.

The next day, I observed students at lunch in the project area between first and second grade. I followed the teacher as she led students to the multipurpose area to get lunch and then return to the project area to eat. The room was full, and the noise level rose and fell as the aides moved about, urging students to be quiet. Two aides and a custodian were present. They issued milk, made change, and helped children open their milk. As I left the project area and moved into the adjoining classroom where a lesson was being taught, the noise was noticeable, and I wondered if it distracted the teacher. However, the lesson involved an individual activity, and neither teacher nor students seemed to notice.

The opening days of school were pleasant; teachers were busy teaching, and students were actively involved in learning. A consistent sense of order and purpose prevailed. Richard said his goal was to keep things moving and solve problems as they came up. He devoted a significant amount of time fine-tuning the project area lunch arrangement, the success of which varied with the age group. I walked with him to the first- and second-grade project area to supervise lunch, and he stated, "First-grade teachers have made some suggestions that will help with lunch in the project areas." For example, the four teachers on the first-grade team decided that one of them would eat with children on an alternating basis to help with supervision. One of them told me it would also help them know their children better, even though it might reduce the time for their own lunch. This change allowed Richard to move all but one aide to another project area, which helped overall supervision.

In visiting with the third-grade team, one teacher described a conflict associated with helping students at lunch. "With lunch in the project area, I am cutting it close on my own lunch. I have been getting ten to twelve minutes. It may be due to handing out milk to children." She hoped this problem might be addressed by an aide instead of her.

More than seven hundred children moved through the lunch process every day, and the number of staff available to supervise and clean up varied. For example, aides, largely attached to secretarial functions, were sometimes engaged in other duties that prevented or delayed arrival. At times, it was not possible for custodians to clean the area after lunch completely, which limited the use of project areas for instruction. And importantly, because Richard was involved in the supervision of lunch, he could not focus on other things that constantly encroached on his to-do list.

By shuffling tables among project areas, children were usually able to find a seat. However, upon occasion, teachers brought chairs from class areas to ease crowding. Richard's participation in lunch took several forms. With younger children, he often moved around, talking quietly and praising students. At times, he would be firm, requesting quiet, with reminders to remain seated. He frequently told children that quiet was necessary because teachers were teaching nearby. On occasion, he made his point by saying, "If you don't get quiet, you may have consequences—lose some playtime." But most of the time, his behavior was more like that of a grandfather: firm, friendly, and approachable.

As the architect of the project area lunch arrangement, Richard wanted to give teachers a duty-free lunch and make the multipurpose area available for physical education teachers. He was committed to making the plan work, but balancing all the elements, including his own involvement in the process, was a challenge. At the conclusion of lunch on September 11, Richard spoke of his effort to cope: "I am planning by the month. The biggest problem is attending to details like furniture [had to move tables around] and custodial work schedules during lunch. The principal has no help and must do everything."

Later that day, I joined Richard as he addressed a discipline matter. Over the weekend, a student had climbed to the roof of the school and found several kickballs, which he shared with his friends. Richard talked with the boy, who admitted what he'd done, and discussed the issue with the sixth-grade team. "What do your recommend we do?" he asked. "The boy and his father are coming in tomorrow. I also think you should talk with your classes about getting on the roof not being a good thing to do."

One team member said, "We need to do something so he knows it's serious."

Another teacher said, "Maybe have him stay after school and work at some dirty job and not do work that's fun."

In thinking about the time he and teachers would have to devote to working on the matter, Richard proposed an alternative. "Maybe we should put the punishment responsibility on the father so we don't have to monitor it—we will have to organize time from our schedule, and if we don't, it won't be meaningful." Team members agreed. He told the group that he would tell the father that the roof had to be checked for damage and mention the cost of ball replacement. The team agreed that the father should be responsible because the act happened on a weekend. He later told his counselor he intended to have parents handle situations like this in the future so school personnel didn't have to be responsible.

September 14: Open House

During parent coffees, Richard discussed how open space would be used at Highcroft as he responded to the apparent disconnect between their experience in traditional classrooms and newer approaches to school design. Their notions about open space were colored by their prior experience and reinforced by negative views held by critics. So public perceptions preceded the opening of school as parents maintained a wait-and-see attitude.

I attended the open house September 14, and I was surprised with the turnout. It was crowded. Richard informed me that approximately one and a half parents represented each of the 725 pupils enrolled at Highcroft. Elementary school parent nights were always well attended throughout the school district, but the estimated twelve hundred parents who attended Highcroft was not anticipated.

If anyone was concerned about open space, it was not apparent. Parents smiled and expressed appreciation to teachers and Richard for the smooth opening to the school year. Given the history of open-space schools, one might have expected considerable dissent, and teachers were both surprised and appreciative of the parents' response. A first-grade teacher described her experience during the evening: "I was talking with a parent last night about open space. He had come from California, where open space had been a failure, and he was expecting the same thing here. I assured him that it would be OK and it was. He said it [open space] wasn't really as open as he had thought."

During the evening, I walked through her classroom when she was demonstrating how the divider panels could be moved. She was small in stature but moved the panels with aplomb. In various ways, other teachers talked about openness from the perspective of how it was utilized in support of teaching and learning. Another teacher said, "Parents were told the building would be built according to plan during the coffees" that Richard held. She believed it enhanced his credibility.

The day after open house, a parent made an unannounced visit and walked into a third-grade class to see for herself whether it was as quiet as her daughter said it was. On the way out, she told Richard's secretary, "It was so quiet you could hear a pin drop."

Richard was pleased with the response from parents. "There

were no negative comments. People saw that open construction was the way I said it would be."

Ongoing Adjustments to Lunch Procedure

As the year progressed, it was clear that lunch in project areas required continued attention. Ongoing issues of supervision, noise, and cleanup predominated, all of which required considerable attention from Richard. In late September, I entered the first- and second-grade project area, where the first-grade teachers were sitting with children during lunch. A custodian and an aide were also present as teachers opened milk containers and talked quietly with the children. The presence of teachers made a significant difference, and everything was quiet and orderly. One of the teachers said the lunch procedure wasn't ideal, but teachers wanted to do their part to make it work. Teachers throughout the building echoed this attitude as they recognized the imperfection of the process.

A second-grade teacher raised questions about lunch in project areas. She explained that during lunch, project areas were not available for instructional use. Since custodians were responsible for cleaning all four lunch locations, they were not always clean enough to allow project areas to be used later in the day. She felt that it wouldn't change because of Richard's decision regarding lunch. Later I saw the reading specialist walking to the opposite end of the building to a drinking fountain. She said she couldn't use the drinking fountain in the project area near her office because "fountains in project areas are a mess."

A few days later, I visited the fifth- and sixth-grade project area, which was supervised by three aides monitoring arriving sixth graders. The noise grew as they occupied the area. I sat in an adjoining classroom as a teacher presented a lesson on large numbers. The moment was captured in my field notes:

It is very difficult for me to hear. A girl about five feet from me gives an answer, but I cannot hear it. The students seem to hear, as does the teacher. Maybe it's because the child is facing the teacher—or kids can block out noise. But it distracted me. (Field notes, September 9, 1978)

I returned to the project area as the noise escalated when more sixth graders entered. In a loud voice, one of the aides said, "OK, boys and girls, you're much too loud. You must be quiet, OK? Thank you." Richard had been trying to educate the aides and custodians to be more vocal, but on this particular day, only one of the three aides didn't say anything. Earlier one of the sixth-grade teachers got the children's attention, stating, "You are much too loud. There is no shouting or loud talking from one table to the next. Talk quietly with those at your table." Her voice was elevated and authoritative as she tried to get compliance. When I spoke with her later, she said the noise level was giving her a headache. The staff associated with lunch supervision, or proximity to project areas during lunch, were annoyed by the din but remained confident that it would eventually improve.

The next day, I accompanied Richard to fourth-grade lunch, where children were engaged in very loud talk. He switched off the lights and said, "Boys and girls, boys and girls, listen to me. You are all talking too loud. You don't have to talk that loud. You can hear each other just as well by talking more quietly. We don't want to disturb others, OK?" Three aides were there cleaning tables and dismissing children who were done. The noise diminished to whispers, and Richard switched on the lights as we left. Richard smiled as he patted a boy on the shoulder, which seemed to say silently, "I still like you, but I need everyone's cooperation."

Richard later returned to help with arriving fifth graders. There was considerable noise, and Richard said, "You must keep your voices down." He wasn't angry, but he didn't smile as he tried to win their cooperation. The noise subsided and then returned as more children entered. There weren't enough chairs, so Richard gathered a few from the adjoining class area. A few boys were standing as they ate their lunches. The noise level was acute, and Richard said, "OK, the next person who talks gets five." He held up five fingers. "If I go like this"—again he held up five fingers—"you sit for five minutes." The project area became very quiet as Richard surveyed the scene. "If I go like this"—he flashed five fingers twice in succession—"you sit for ten minutes."

When he observed a girl he suspected of talking, he said, "OK, you—yes, you," flashing five fingers at her.

The girl appeared bewildered and said, "I didn't say anything."

Richard responded, "Were you moving your lips?"

She reluctantly said yes to moving her lips, and Richard, seemingly aware he had made his point, said, "Well, OK, I'll let you off the hook this time." As he moved around the room he "flashed five" at two other students. His manner was stern and unsmiling as he moved about. The atmosphere was quiet, and aides were busy cleaning tables.

Richard modeled the behavior he expected from custodians and aides who supervised lunch. He expended considerable time and energy in his attempt to instill assertiveness in stating expectations.

On another occasion, I followed him to the sixth-grade project area, where he found three girls finishing lunch. With eyes wide with amazement, he said, "Are you girls all that's left of the sixth-grade lunch group?" They indicated that they were. Richard was gleeful with this news, saying, "Very good. Very good."

He began talking with me about his efforts to refine lunch procedures. "We have fine-tuned lunch. The aides have known what they're supposed to do, but we have been working so hard on the procedure that aides have felt a little timid about enforcing rules. We talked about that this morning," referring to regular meetings he scheduled to discuss behavior management techniques. Richard understood that child behavior was related to age and grade level, and he taught his supervisors to adjust their stance according to the maturity of the kids. It was time well spent on his part. Consequently, lunch behavior improved, but it was far from perfect as the aides tried to use their voices and movements around the room to maintain quiet.

Toward the end of September, several picnic tables were placed near the west entrance to the multipurpose area, thereby providing a welcome respite from eating lunch exclusively in project spaces. The children loved being outside, and Richard was happy to have an alternative. However, he soon discovered bees and other insects attracted to the food. A few children were victims of stings. One day at the beginning of lunch, I asked three aides why they were going to the project areas rather than outside to supervise and they retorted, "Too many bees!" Lunch in the picnic area resumed in a few days, after Richard made a few changes in the way custodians cleaned the area. After a bit of insect spraying and extra care about food disposal, outside lunch resumed.

Without Richard's attention to lunch supervision, the entire scheme could have fallen apart. In schools where lunch occurs in a traditional lunchroom, where teachers are expected to eat lunch with their children, a principal has an hour or so to attend to other things that needed attention. Time is always a factor in the life of a principal, but Richard was committed to a duty-free lunch for his teachers. He expected much, and he wanted them to have the opportunity to eat without interruption. A summary of the impact of lunch procedures as it relates to teachers and the principal is shown in figure 8.

The work of teachers often extends into the evening, when papers are graded and lessons fine-tuned. A teacher is on the receiving end of the politicized emphasis on student achievement as measured by state and national tests. There may be a need for high stakes testing, but it takes a toll on teachers who are on the front line of the process. The time demands on teachers influenced Richard in numerous ways, such as the unspoken bargain he had with teachers regarding duty-free lunch. As a team, everyone had a role in making the organization work. Richard often quoted Franklin Roosevelt, who, at the height of the Great Depression said, "Everyone has to do their part" in restoring the economic health of the nation. At Highcroft, Richard was doing his part, and everyone—children, teachers, and parents—recognized it.

Figure 8
Impact of Lunch Procedure

```
DUTY FREE              TEACHER
LUNCH FOR    TIME FOR TEAM    APPRECIATION
TEACHERS     PLANNING         OF RICHARD'S
                              EFFORTS

RICHARD                       PROGRESS AS A
SUPERVISES       GOALS        COLLABORATIVE
LUNCH                         SCHOOL

COMMITMENT   ACCEPTANCE OF    REDUCED
OF RICHARD'S  ADDED STRESS    FLEXIBILITY IN
TIME                          RICHARD'S
                              SCHEDULE
```

One afternoon I arrived at Highcroft with the intention of speaking with Richard. One of his office staff said, "Didn't you see him mowing the lawn?" When I returned to the schoolyard, I saw Richard, dressed in bib overalls and an engineer's cap, driving a lawn tractor. He was all smiles and waved to me as he passed. Later that day, I asked him why he was doing a task normally done by district maintenance staff, and he said, "I want the kids to see that we are capable of contributing to the appearance of school and grounds." He and his staff planted trees and flowers as well as built some of the playground equipment. Children were often involved in these improvement projects.

When the district staff bulletin came out September 26, the search for a new superintendent was announced. Search brochures and accompanying applications were to be sent to each school for inspection by interested staff members. The previous superintendent had been in his position for several years and was well known for his support for open-plan schools. During his tenure, two open-plan middle schools, a high school, and three elementary schools had opened. From 1960 to1970, open-plan schools were constructed throughout the United States and were not always well received by parents. A report from the Florida State Department of Education (George 1975) discussed several problems associated with open schools but also reported their potential and said they should not be dismissed out of hand. However, in announcing the search for a new superintendent, the school district was changing its point of emphasis. The shift in focus would eventually become clear in the mission of a new superintendent who arrived four years later.

September 29: Richard Overfelt Recognition Day

I arrived at Highcroft before school began on September 29 and heard a public address announcement from Richard's secretary, requesting the staff to assemble in the multipurpose area. Richard was seated on a bench, and all the teachers were lined up to give him kisses and hugs. He was surprised. The social committee, headed by one of the kindergarten teachers, had orchestrated the event. It was a culmination of a week of behind-the-scenes activity where children planned something special for Richard.

Kindergartners made books with a cover picture of a man made out of geometric symbols. The children named him "High Crofty." Richard entered the room and received their books and a chant they did in unison: "Highcroft is a great place to be!" they shouted. Richard sat on the floor and unwrapped the booklets, holding up each one so the children could see. He admired each picture and said, "I'm going keep these booklets in my office, and when you get to sixth grade, I want you to come in and see them. You've made me feel very special today. Do you know why Highcroft is a special place? It's because of the good students, good teachers, and good parents we have. Thank you very much, boys and girls."

The recognition moved to sixth grade, and all four classes gathered around him as he sat on a high stool. One of the sixth-grade teachers thanked him for making Highcroft a great school. Various students came forward to give him an autograph book signed by all the children. Richard kissed the girls and hugged the boys, stating, "It's OK for two boys who like each other to hug."

Another teacher presented him with a sixth-grade T-shirt, which he wore. Richard responded, "I want to thank you all very much for making me feel very special. Whenever you're nice to someone else, it causes them to be nice. Kindness brings out kindness."

Another teacher concluded his presentation with, "The kids want to know you better."

Richard responded, "Yes, you're right, and I'm going to be doing more of that [visiting each pod] in the future."

Every grade level contributed to the recognition of Richard throughout the day. Carnations came from a third-grade team, along with hugs and kisses. Another third-grade class arrived at his office door to sing a song. They couldn't all fit in his office, so he moved to the hall. The fifth-grade team lined up their students, who thanked him for making their school so nice. Like other classes during the day, they gave him books made in class. Richard smiled throughout all the displays of affection, and his remarks were heartfelt. The children were well mannered and disciplined in their presentations. Carnations from every corner of the building continued to arrive at his office, eventually forming a huge bouquet.

As the end of the day approached, Richard arrived in the fifth-grade pod to receive recognition Each teacher lined up their presenters, who told him, "Thank you for making Highcroft such a great place." They gave him books they'd made.

He smiled and responded gently, "I will look at your books, and I will enjoy them. When you return for a visit when you're in high school, come by and see what we did this day. It makes me feel good inside because of what you and your teachers have done for me. It will help me through those days when I get down, and I have days like that; we all do. You're a good group of kids. You're kind to each other."

With that said, the pod erupted in applause, and one of the children yelled, "Hurrah for Dr. Overfelt."

The recognition from teachers and students was moving and revealed Richard's sensitive interior. He reacted to the attention by saying it would sustain him at those times when he felt down. The comment was unusual for Richard, who always put a smile on everyone he encountered. In an interview months earlier, I'd asked him if he ever felt depressed, and he said that during the Depression, people sometimes felt blue, but they addressed it by getting busy and doing something positive. During the Depression, people were prone to work their way through difficult emotional psychological situations. That was typical of life in Duncans Bridge as the Depression deepened.

Amid all the accolades, Richard told me he had to meet with a group of room mothers in the multipurpose area, and I attended with him. As we arrived, I saw a large group of mothers just finishing their business, waiting for Richard to speak. I told Richard that I hoped they remained friendly, and we both laughed.

Much to my surprise, when he introduced me, he said, "Wayne asked me who you were. Wayne said, 'I hope they remain friendly.'" This was followed by laughter from the mothers. He went on: "I also hope you remain friendly." Again there was much laughter.

Richard was wearing the sixth-grade T-shirt over his shirt and tie. It was a tight fit, which accentuated his abdomen. He sat down in the center of the group and began speaking. One of the mothers told him, "Stand up. We can't hear you."

He responded, "That means you're all going to have to listen better and I'm going to have to talk louder." Whenever he was speaking to any group, whether parents, teachers, children, or professional colleagues, he never stood. I did not fully grasp why this was the case. Was he a bit timid in front of groups? Did he want to avoid others seeing him as too dominant? Or was it merely more comfortable for him? It may have been motivated by beliefs regarding leadership where everyone was an equal member of the group.

He thanked them for sending good kids to school, followed by other comments: "Homes are very important. You are the best teachers your children will ever have. The kids are really working hard. Most of them are trying to be courteous. We hear so many children say thank you—even the lunch ladies say so. Your kids are good persons. They are working hard on talking quietly." Richard concluded with an invitation. "This is an open school, and you don't need an invitation to visit. Come anytime."

Afterward, he paused to talk with three room mothers who were counting money in the multipurpose area. He thanked them for all they had done and gave each a hug and a kiss. Richard was unlike most school administrators who maintained social distance with children and parents. Natural gestures of affection were the norm for Richard in working with everyone.

Later the staff made a presentation that took the format of Academy Awards. One of the teachers on the social committee served as mistress of ceremonies, and three other teachers acted as presenters. Their presentations were made with appropriate flourish as names were drawn from a coffee can that had been "held in great security." Of course, Richard won in each category. The first two presentations were the "Richie Awards," two plaques made out of paper. The third was a wooden plaque with an engraved brass plate stating, "Highcroft Ridge loves Richard Overfelt." Richard expressed an emotional thank-you to everyone but couldn't say more without shedding tears.

As the day of recognition ended, I found myself reflecting on all the accolades he received and his heartfelt response to their demonstrations. He was visibly moved by everyone's efforts to thank him. He was always appreciative and calm in working with people, but on this day, he seemed more relaxed and, at least for a moment, free of the tension of daily operations. His voice was filled with sentiment and sincere gratitude. The fond words he spoke to children and staff likely made them feel special too. It was the kind of day that sustains people involved with the demanding and often complex work of schooling. Recognition of children and teachers helps to establish a positive school climate.

Formal Patterns of Staff and Pupil Recognition

Highcroft had a unique approach to recognizing children, staff, and parents. One form was a simple "happy gram" teachers used to recognize students for good work. It was a half sheet of paper showing a newsboy holding a newspaper where an inscription was written. It was titled "Highcroft Ridge Happy Gram" and was used to recognize achievements and nice things people did for each other. More often than not, when they recognized a student or an entire class, Richard was notified, and he invited them to his office to underscore the positive thing they had done. When two or three children were involved, the meeting was held in his office; but when an entire class was recognized, Richard stood at his door offering words of appreciation. His demeanor was as usual—low-key, smiling, and calm in making comments. Instances of recognition usually required two hours or more to complete, and they represented Richard's commitment to recognition of children and teachers.

In early November, I observed Richard as he recognized individual children recommended by teachers who made nice comments about something they accomplished. The gathering was held in the "rocking chair" [conference] room as Richard sat on an antique church bench. He spoke with each one individually, saying, "I've been hearing some nice things about you. Mrs. Jones said you did very well on a social studies test. She said you use all your talents all the time and that you are a good worker. You've had a good start, and I know you are going to have a good year, OK?" He'd give the child a pat on the back. The child would smile and thank him. "OK," Richard would say. "We'll be seeing you." Then another child came into the room for her turn in the limelight.

Richard's office decor was unique and reflected his origins in northeast Missouri. It was quaint but attractive. A park bench holding a furry dog was along one wall. A low table with a lamp was in one corner, bordered by two rocking chairs. The wall near the door had a built-in desk with cabinets above it. The entire setting was decorated with pictures of country schoolchildren playing a game of crack the whip and a schoolmarm teaching in a one-room school in the 1800s. A painting of Woodlawn, Richard's first school, had a prominent place on a side wall. Other items like a horse shoe mounted on a plaque, an old rake without a handle, other pictures with barn board frames, and an old school bell were among the many antiques in the room.

There were also practical things like a large piece of white butcher paper taped to a wall for making quick notations, a bulletin board with lists of volunteers, schedules, district telephone numbers, and emergency procedures. His desk held an antique wooden box with a bunch of pencils, along with two folders marked "Custodian" and "Needs." The collective impact of this unique setting prompted an entry in my field notes: "This room is organized and inhabited by a person who values the past. It is a warm place where rustic picture frames match the brown desktop and chairs." A few weeks later, I observed Richard's wife, Myra, hanging wallpaper that added her personal touch. Myra was a quiet but pronounced presence in supporting Richard and doing nice things for the teachers and staff.

Another form of recognition was the "rose award," a simple drawing of a red rose with a place for comments. It was intended as recognition for special effort or unique accomplishments. In earning the award, the recipient sat on the "rose rug" as Richard intoned remarks in his typical folksy style. Teachers sometimes received the award and were seated on the rose rug during staff meetings. Occasionally, children and even parents were recipients. Recognition was a ritual at Highcroft, and the rose rug was worn thin by hundreds of students, teachers, and staff members who received the award.

The Parent Volunteer Program Is Launched

School volunteer programs can be good or bad, depending on leadership and the degree of organization. As a former country schoolteacher, Richard experienced a close relationship between school and community, where people felt an ownership and sense of responsibility for its success. When planned and implemented effectively, a volunteer program can promote positive community relations and public willingness to support school tax levies and bond issues. In the event these elements are missing, a volunteer program may be marginally successful at best.

Richard had an expansive model in mind as he searched for a leader of the volunteer program. He wanted an organization that was broader in scope than traditional arrangements, such as room mothers who helped organize class parties. Richard looked for someone capable of mounting such an effort. Interestingly, he found a person who did not have children at Highcroft but had extensive experience in leading volunteer programs in other states. His new volunteer coordinator understood what Richard wanted and immediately put plans in action in early October. Two subsequent meetings identified various volunteer categories as she and several parents prepared and mailed five hundred letters to homes in the Highcroft attendance area. From the 250 responses, a foundation of 210 volunteers was identified for thirteen categories shown below:

       Art Appreciation
       Clerical Aides
       Community School Planning

Gardening and Grounds
Health Room
Junior Great Books
Library Aides
Lunchroom Aides
Music Appreciation
Nature Study Area
Newsletter
Room Mothers
Special Courses
Tutors

The list was published in the October edition of the *Highcroft Ridge Hotline Reporter*, with the name and telephone number of each group chairperson. The largest category was Room Mothers, and Art Appreciation was one of the smallest. It was a significant response and even included people with full-time jobs. Each category was staffed by a parent as chairperson, and most categories had two or three.

I interviewed the leader of the volunteer program in late October to discuss her perceptions. She described Richard as a marvelous man who was "demanding and giving," well organized, and knew what he wanted to accomplish. She believed the response from parents was due largely to Richard and the teachers who'd attended the multitude of parent coffees earlier in the spring. "Richard made himself available to parents, and parents spread the word to at least five other parents. The coffees gave people a good first impression of him. The fact that he brought along teachers helped a lot because they conversed at the level of the parents." The twenty-six coffees required more energy than Richard or teachers may have recognized at the time, but they had a huge impact with regard to building parent involvement.

CHAPTER 11
The Pursuit of Collaboration

Assumptions about Team Teaching

Collaboration at Highcroft rested on the belief that teaching is enhanced when individual teachers work together in sharing their knowledge and experience. It further suggested that discourse among like-minded people is perfected within an atmosphere of cooperation, patience, and mutual respect. At its best, team teaching can have synergistic effects, where collaboration leads to more effective academic outcomes. Simply put, to be an effective team, individual teachers should be confident about their interpersonal skills and willing to contribute their ideas for the benefit of the team. It takes time and patience in forming an effective team. Less constructive issues may interfere with progress. In the worst-case scenario, isolation, negative sentiment, and rigidity may lead to token participation, or worse, team dissolution. Therefore, effective teamwork requires self-monitoring and oversight by team members, a principal, and others who could provide assistance if needed.

Through fall and early winter, I observed teachers in team meetings and impromptu conversations in the lunchroom, work areas, and hallways, and I was struck by the familiarity and ease of these encounters. The informality of social interactions was important in influencing a positive school climate. I wondered if it was a true reality or a facade intended for public consumption. What did the details of teamwork reveal about daily routines?

On October 9, I attended a meeting with Richard and his specialist regarding the Houghton Mifflin program. Second-grade teachers had shared frustrations with him regarding time required for extensive data collecting and recording, and he sought her ideas about possible adjustments to reduce the burden. At the April planning session, she gave a lengthy presentation on the reading program, including details about grouping, reading levels, and selection of appropriate supplementary materials. When she asked for questions, there were none. Everyone indicated their approval. However, when school began and the program was implemented, teachers were exposed to the reality of record keeping and reporting. If it was just one program they had to contend with, the problem would have been manageable. But within the context of all curricula, lesson planning, team planning, and school-related information requests, teachers were feeling overwhelmed.

Richard asked her, "Can any part of it [record keeping] be cut out?"

She responded, "No, because it all has aspects of skill development measured on a pre-post [test] basis. So if a teacher doesn't follow the program and mark each child's progress, then the next teacher won't know where to place the kid."

"So you're saying it can't be changed so that parts of the program are deleted," Richard said.

"That's right."

Richard continued to probe: "What if once every couple of weeks, the teachers didn't do the reading program but did something else?" The tone of this exchange was amicable as both tried to find a level of agreement.

She said, "Sure, like a whole class project on fairy tales involving puppetry or just reading for appreciation. But I don't see how that would provide a teacher with more time for record keeping, though. It could prevent their files from getting any thicker, and that might help them catch up."

Richard acknowledged that it might be helpful, and the reading specialist recommended that it be brought up at a staff meeting.

A week after his meeting with the reading specialist, I spoke with Richard about record keeping, especially in reading. He said, "Everyone feels burdened from time to time, especially in an elementary school with so much going on." He said that one of the more outspoken members of the second-grade team had brought it to his attention. "I talked with all of them the other day. I told them not to get a big list of things to do. It won't hurt the program if they break the routine."

Based on his discussion with the reading specialist, Richard told the team it could be adapted so they didn't have to read every day of the week, which would, at the very least, make record keeping more manageable.

In talking with me later, Richard said, "Teachers were used to teaching programs rather than kids. Some kids in second grade were pretested and started on first-grade reading materials because kids were grouped. This was a concern for some teachers because it meant they would have to explain to parents why a second-grade child who was in a second-grade reader at a previous school was now placed in first-grade material at Highcroft." Therefore, the issue was not just time required for record keeping but also having to face parents, who found it difficult to accept the placement of their child in a less advanced level. This was not a problem for first-grade teachers, who started from zero in their pretesting and placement of children.

Statewide Testing

The origin of state-sponsored academic testing began in the early 1970s in the wake of public disenchantment with the Vietnam War, political upheaval during the Watergate period, and a general dissatisfaction with the financing of public education. Previously, it had been common for school districts to use standardized tests in one form or another to gather data about student performance. However, the public expressed concerns about students not learning the basics. During this period, state departments of education designed tests to measure essential skills that followed the pedagogy of validity and reliability rubrics that included voluntary field-testing. In Missouri, the instrument was called the Basic Essential Skills Test, or BEST, which was introduced to a sampling of school districts statewide in 1977, and Parkway was one of the districts in the sample.

The results of the first administration of BEST were reported in the district staff bulletin early October 1978. The first iteration of BEST was aimed at eighth graders, and the results placed Parkway in the top 10 percent of school districts in the sample. The results were not unusual for Parkway students, who consistently scored well on standardized tests and college entry examinations. The results were accompanied by an announcement from the Missouri Department of Education that BEST would be mandatory for all eighth graders in the future. Questions about the nature of the test, its content, and the possible relationship to state funding of schools began to appear. It was the beginning of an emphasis on high stakes testing that has expanded as an influence on curricula, school district assessment programs, and school funding. Eventually, newer versions of BEST included applications for elementary and high school. Questions proliferated about what constitutes a basic skill, the inclusion of assessments of higher order thinking skills, and the intrusion of an additional responsibility managed by teachers.

The impact of basic skills testing did not have an immediate effect on elementary schools. However, as state testing progressed, new iterations of BEST eventually involved elementary children. As principal at Highcroft, Richard was vocal in his dissent of high stakes testing, which he believed was yet another distraction to teaching and learning. While he could not opt out of the program, he was not an advocate, and his views about the intrusion of state testing programs were widely known and not always appreciated by supervisors.

Reading Program Adjustments

During the monthly planning sessions earlier in the year, time was given to every curriculum in the Highcroft program. The selection of a supplier, supplementary materials, assessments, and schedules was discussed in considerable detail. The narrative highlighted deliberations of curricula, and reading demanded considerable attention. Considering the extensive details involved in teaching reading, teachers were very attentive because they would be involved in recommending a program.

A lively discussion of the reading program occurred during the October 17 staff meeting. Later that day, Richard met with the first-grade team to address specific questions they raised. There was no small talk, and a male member of the team began by asking Richard to explain "instructional level." Richard was a bit surprised by the sudden onset of his question, and a degree of irritation was noticeable in Richard's response. "Remember what I told you when I met with you individually? You told me you wanted to meet as a team. So that's what we're doing. A new system for reporting pupil progress [in reading] was studied for a year, and now we have it, and now we're trying to find ways to circumvent it." He didn't appear to be angry, but he projected a bit of frustration with a problem he had been dealing with since school began.

Undaunted, the teacher posed another question: "If a kid was not through [expected book], should he be marked below grade level?

Especially since that book is marginal in its importance. When do they finally get marked at grade level?"

Richard allowed ample time for him to state his question and then said, "If they get to the book beyond Honeycombs [one book within a series of Houghton-Mifflin books], and they probably won't, and the Houghton Mifflin consultant said they won't, then maybe Honeycombs would be our measure of being at grade level by the end of the year." Richard was at his best in moments like this. A decision was made that seemed to cut through the fog of uncertainty that existed at the start of the meeting.

Another teacher raised a question about the kinds of comments they should include: "Should we have negative comments?"

Richard replied, "No ... only through needs improvement in categories shown."

Another teacher sought clarification, saying, "So are we supposed to mark pupil progress and not achievement?" Richard told them to mark only progress. The teacher then turned to team members and asked if they had other questions.

A fourth member of the team said, "Where do we make additional comments or suggestions?"

Richard told them to put their comments on the back of the conference form, adding, "Please be very honest about personal work habits. This is very important at conference time, especially when there have been problems." He told the group that first- and second-grade teachers set the tone for conferences.

There were a few other questions about how to mark PE, art, and music, followed by a summary comment from the teacher who initially spoke. "We just wanted you to help us with our thinking on this."

"I appreciate that," Richard said, "but if this group decides something else, that will be OK. Try to end every conference by saying, 'Is there anything else you would like to ask?' That way, they [parents] can't go away saying that we didn't ask them. Put the responsibility on them."

They again thanked him for his time, and Richard told them, "You don't have to say that, because I'm no busier than you. In fact, I'm not as busy as you are."

Teachers were committed to the mission of Highcroft outlined by Richard at the first planning session in January 1978, and it was evident in their reactions to Richard's leadership and their enthusiasm for the new school. In their study of an innovative elementary school, Smith and Keith (1971) found varying degrees of "true belief," a kind of fanatical faith among the staff during the period of socialization to the new school. At Highcroft, elements of true belief existed beyond initial planning meetings through the opening of school. Teachers with previous connections with Richard helped to diffuse a sense of commitment to newer staff members. Planning sessions became the means for developing the norms and sentiments typical of a collaborative organization. The degree of success in this process was manifested in the opening of the school in August 1978.

Gradual Steps toward Collaboration

In mid-October, I spoke with a member of the third-grade team with prior experience working with Richard and who talked about the patience required for teamwork. "Some of us have been strategically placed on teams, but we can't just tell others how to do things."

An experienced teacher on the sixth-grade team joined the conversation, saying, "That's right. We have to let them come to conclusions for themselves. The math program, for example. I hated it ... I have had experience with it, but I couldn't tell the others on the team that. I had to wait until they recognized that for themselves, and it takes time."

During the months of planning, the idea of collaboration was not addressed in any formal way, but it was clearly in Richard's thinking as he interviewed teachers and in the personal and interpersonal qualities teachers possessed. He believed teachers should first be good persons and, second, technically sound. The degree of collaboration required for cooperative decision-making was, in Richard's view, an essential foundation. The degree of success in creating a collaborative school rested on the selection of teachers who were, in Richard's hierarchy of attributes, good persons.

Changing the direction of the conversation, the third-grade teacher stated, "I would like to use the project areas more for art and science, but noisy activities disturb the class next door. And showing a film out on the steps [leading from hall to pods] sounded great, but when we [third-grade team] do this, the fourth grade watches too." Teachers also spoke about the intensity of meetings for mainstreaming, recording and reporting data on reading, the spelling program, and parent conferences that required a significant time commitment they found difficult to manage.

Richard was always available to listen to concerns, reassuring them that they didn't have to do everything. He provided some relief in terms of reading, and teachers helped themselves by using open space wisely for large group sessions, which gave a modicum of time for other team members to catch up on work. However, teachers were uncertain about what else could be done to arrest the strain.

On October 29, the daily routine was set aside for the Halloween parade. The event had been planned weeks ago, and the excitement grew as the day drew near. Teachers wore outlandish costumes, and Richard, at the head of the parade, was dressed in a clown suit. At 2 p.m., everyone lined up behind a police escort and followed a circular route along several blocks near the school. Lots of parents and children lined the street and shouted their approval. The event concluded with a party at school, and everyone participated, including Richard and the teachers. The celebration was the first of what would become an annual event. Everyone then quickly returned to business as usual.

By the end of October, most teams had acclimated to team

planning and were working collaboratively. The sixth-grade team members had worked through their individual differences and seemed to enjoy working together. During their team planning, they often laughed, made jokes, and exhibited an easy give-and-take as they worked on instructional issues that carried over to implementing lessons with students. The fourth-grade team was functioning well but continued to work on communications. The fifth-grade teams had become a smooth working unit. Some members of the first- and second-grade teams were more reserved and others more vocal, but these differences didn't appear to interfere with planning.

It was Richard's habit to meet with teams on a regular basis. In mid-October, I attended one of his meetings with the third-grade team in the relaxed atmosphere of his office. His meetings always began with a variation of the statement "Tell me something I should be doing that I'm not doing. Pick an area you are teaming on and tell me how you feel about it."

One teacher spoke positively about the reading program. They discussed the range of pupil reading levels and the continual focus on pacing themselves to address student needs. They all agreed that data gathering and recording were demanding but manageable. Richard talked about avoiding labeling students as they worked with diverse reading groups.

One of the teachers offered a positive view about reading in her advanced group, who worked effectively on supplementary reading materials. She said, "I feel good about it. I'm pacing myself."

Another teacher followed with, "What she's saying is that she's good." The other teachers smiled and chimed in with agreement. They discussed the range of abilities in slow, average, and high groupings and the need to avoid labeling students.

Another teacher talked about a project she was attempting that would reinforce reading. "I'm trying to set up some activity centers, like SRAs on language arts. We need more tables, and the project area needs to be closed in." Although the use of the project area for lunch was prominent in faculty conversation, suggestions about altering the space was unusual and perhaps an indication of frustration.

Richard paused and then offered an idea: "What if we placed a shag carpet on walls on each end [of the project area] to absorb noise?" It was not clear exactly how this might look or significantly reduce noise, and it didn't receive further consideration.

Richard followed with another idea: "At some point in the future, it would be good to sit down with the fourth grade and check the schedule to find slots where you could use the room without interfering with each other ... This can be worked out."

Teachers had an opportunity to speak, and Richard listened without judgment as he made a few final remarks. "Thanks to you all. I'm glad you're excited about the reading program. I think it's a good management system ... It takes a lot to make it work."

During the meeting, there was no indication of communication difficulties brewing within the third-grade team. However, as fall progressed, Richard became aware of the mounting stress within the team and attempted to intervene. For the moment, the problems were compartmentalized, but they would eventually evolve as a breakdown in team cooperation.

On another occasion, Richard and I discussed a recent meeting he had with the fourth-grade team. Like other teams, fourth-grade teachers talked about problems or issues related to their grade level. One described a pattern of urinating on the floor in the boys' restroom. The perpetrator was unknown, but they had suspicions and planned to follow up. The team also discussed their dissatisfaction with the way they used the fourth-grade teaching space and the desire to experiment by moving partitions, allowing large group instruction. Richard supported their plan and its potential for creating additional planning time for individual teachers. As the session concluded, a teacher noted that the project area lunch arrangement was working well. Progress was directly related to the extraordinary investment of Richard's oversight and intervention.

A common concern among all teams was the timely duplication of materials they prepared for classroom use. Originally, Richard assigned this work to aides in the office. Highcroft teachers were innovators motivated to develop activities used immediately. Consequently, their reach outran the production capacity of office personnel. In recognizing the problem, Richard ordered additional duplication equipment for teacher access in their work areas. He never questioned or argued about implementing a change that supported instructional planning.

Increasing Stress

When school opened and the serious business of lesson development began, teachers were still acclimating to each other and the processes required for effective teaming. There was no question that initial planning sessions helped teachers become acquainted and engage in various decisions that were needed, but the capacity for effective teaming takes time, and it cannot be rushed. Typically, teams of teachers draw from the instructional strengths each possesses when decisions regarding the assignment of curricular units are made. In this process, teachers express their interests for preparing units, including supplemental materials, that other team members will need in order to introduce the unit to students. Teamwork has many benefits, but shared decisions about who teaches what and when are basic. Third-grade teachers experienced considerable difficulty in following through with curricular commitments. Eventually, they devolved into separate entities, with only occasional cooperation among some members.

The episode began almost from the start of school and continued for the remainder of the school year, taking a toll on the emotional well-being of all involved, including Richard. He devoted considerable time in third grade, working with individual teachers and the team in an effort to help. Richard was an effective principal, but he was not a miracle worker. Teachers on the third-grade team experienced considerable stress that eventually led to health problems for some members of the team. The intransigence of the problem was difficult for Richard, who was usually able to reach constructive outcomes. His reaction was atypical in that his normal open-door stance diminished and teachers found him to be inaccessible. Everyone noticed the change and wanted to help but couldn't. To their credit, the staff did not take sides and remained focused on their own teaching responsibilities. And Richard, in the face of considerable stress, kept things moving.

The situation was moderated somewhat by the first of what would become an annual celebration of Highcroft's founding on January 23, 1978. Teachers spoke about Highcroft successes and recognized important people like Richard and Myra, who had contributed so much to the school. This date was perhaps the most important ritual at Highcroft in highlighting core beliefs: the good person ethic, collaboration, and teamwork and teacher leadership.

For Richard, the second semester had its own unique rhythm of classroom observations and preparation of formal evaluations, culminating in teacher conferences during late winter and spring. Richard's approach to teacher evaluation was unique in his approach. Prior to actual classroom observation, Richard met with individual teachers and requested them to prepare a summary of things they felt good about and plans for the next year. Eventually, he met with the teacher to review the checklist of behaviors on the school district evaluation instrument, but he gave considerable attention to a written addendum (several pages long) that recognized the contributions of each teacher. At the conclusion, Richard invited teachers to select a geranium as part of the recognition. Teachers were gratified with his written remarks, and the geranium became the seal of approval.

A variety of other matters, including those that were unanticipated, demanded his attention. Although Highcroft was sufficiently ready to receive children in August, rolls of carpeting, paint cans, and construction equipment were still visible in the building into the second semester. There were ongoing problems with a leaky roof, and buckets were scattered about on rainy days. From the start of the year, there were continual problems with the heating and cooling system. Richard seemed to be in constant communication with district maintenance people in attempting to solve the problem. He eventually discovered an outside door that didn't fit properly, leaving a gap between the door and the threshold. Whenever the system turned on, it sucked warm air from the room, which was replaced by cold air under the door. Richard often spoke of school construction as a "milk run," where construction workers overlooked, forgot, or purposely ignored important details.

Resiliency is important in the life of an elementary school principal, especially in the unexpected turnover of staff. No matter how diligent and attentive, Richard had to cope with the departure of a fourth-grade teacher whose spouse was transferred. He involved fourth-grade teachers in reading résumés and interviewing candidates, but replacing an experienced teacher who was also a team leader was problematic, and it took several weeks to fill the vacancy.

Managing non-certificated employees also demanded considerable attention from Richard. When he implemented the lunch procedure, custodians and office aides were drawn into the supervision scheme. It was apparent that they had difficulty meeting Richard's expectations, even though he met with them regularly to go over duties. The assignment was greeted with hesitation by some individuals, who complained about duties requiring a "drill sergeant" mentality. One didn't like the "chaotic" nature of the duties, and another resigned because she didn't want to supervise children. Another instructional aide quit for similar reasons, and one was released for poor performance. Finding replacements took time, and in the interim, Richard had to give more attention to lunch supervision. Unanticipated events such as these stretch the limits of resilience.

However, in taking a broad view, much was accomplished despite the challenges of staff turnover and issues of collaboration among grade-level teams. The planning phase that began in January paid huge dividends when school opened, and teachers credited that period as the primary reason behind everything they achieved. They were able to become acquainted with team members' experiences and talents, which led nearly all grade-level teams toward effective collaboration. As the year concluded, most teachers were drained by the experience, but they were gratified by what they achieved as a team.

In June, after school closed, a luncheon was held at a local restaurant, with everyone in attendance. The social committee organized the event, and one of them served as presenter. A member of the committee proposed a toast "to the beginning of Highcroft," and everyone raised a glass. The atmosphere was tinged by the realization that seven teachers would not return the next year for a variety of reasons: change of residence, acceptance of a different teaching position, financial issues, and marriage. However, the cadre of grade-level team leaders remained, along with staff who occupied specializations in counseling, reading, and library. Along with Richard, they represented the core leadership that would influence the continuation of Highcroft the following year.

Following lunch, a few humorous gifts were exchanged, which lightened the mood. The librarian introduced slides of significant events during the year. There were many lighthearted moments, much laughter, and many comments as staff recognized themselves in the retrospective. As her presentation concluded, everyone faced the reality that some of them were leaving. The mood brought forth emotion and tears as they stood together for a photo. Finally, amid hugs and tearful goodbyes, the 1978–1979 school year came to a close.

Summary

The narrative described the evolution of Highcroft Ridge School as a process that began with a planning committee of citizens, school administrators, teachers, and others in identifying the direction for further planning. The superintendent favored the kind of flexible space architecture required to support participative leadership of school programs and services. During his tenure, several open-space buildings were planned and opened amid mixed views of district patrons; many favored schools that were more traditional in construction and instructional practices.

Research on open-space schools did not appear until the 1970s and was limited in both depth and scope. In 1975, Paul George, at the Department of Curriculum and Instruction at the University of Florida, published a paper titled "Ten Years of Open-Space School." The paper reviewed the limited research during that period, which cited the dearth of studies as a serious problem in understanding the impact of open-space schools on teachers, students, and pupil achievement. He observed that many school innovations that appear on the scene are without depth or significance and soon disappear. Others are of such magnitude and permanence that they can be disregarded only at the risk of a loss of effective function of an entire school system. He argued that the open-space school belongs in this category.

His review suggested concerns about noise and other distractions that required research that was more specific. However, he found positive effects on teachers and cooperative team planning, which loomed as an important new direction regarding the professional development of teachers. He also noted evidence to suggest that open-space schools facilitate the growth of positive concepts of self on the part of pupils. In addition, the evidence indicated that such schools provide more opportunities for alternative learning activities, decision-making, independence, and a number of other factors facilitated by open-space schools as they currently functioned.

Highcroft Elementary School was a response to the westward expansion of the school district, with several hundred homes being constructed. The demographics of the community were important: largely white, professional, young (thirties and forties), and upwardly mobile in their worldview. Residents of the Highcroft community chose the location because they were aware of the district's pursuit of excellence. These new residents held high expectations for the education of their children. Some were very skeptical of open space because of direct experiences in other parts of the country, some had a wait-and-see attitude, and the remainder were generally positive about open space. Nevertheless, the community was excited about a neighborhood school and expressed the belief that the quality of a school is ultimately determined by the quality of teachers. These factors influenced specific plans at Highcroft.

The narrative also described the beliefs, values, and goals that Richard brought to the formation of this new entity. While he had limited experience with open flexible space, his ideas and experience suggested a philosophical connection with instructional methods thought to be effective in an open-plan school. His background as a one-room schoolteacher years ago influenced his beliefs about personalized teaching and learning. He had strong attachments to ideas about educating the "total" person through the application of sound human skills in teaching the curriculum. Richard's conception of a school was the antithesis of what most schools are about today. His intention was to honor the individual child by using positive interpersonal skills. By doing so, there existed a possibility that a large school could be made to "feel" smaller. Interpersonal connections during teaching and informal activities with children give impetus to this belief.

Richard's statement of goals, beliefs, values, and sentiments about children resonated with beliefs held by teachers. The discussion of his system of beliefs occurred first during interviews. Those teachers who had worked with him in the past were well aware of his philosophy and were a positive conveyance of his ideas to others. He was consistent in the way he spoke with everyone, including parents, who would form an important support system for the school. Some might argue that Richard was politically motivated in the way he included people, and I suppose there is always a degree of politics in the work of every school leader. However, observation of Richard over a period revealed his commitment to education as a human activity and should occur in a respectful and humane manner. Pupils should be first in planning a school program.

Hence, taken together, Richard's goals, beliefs, sentiments, and ideas formed a platform that Smith and Keith (1971) called "formal doctrine." According to Smith and Keith, the doctrine is a complex combination of a way of thinking that encapsulates a vision for the organization that is concrete and easily noted in dialogue and publication of manuals and other documents. Altogether, the doctrine outlines the direction of an organization. Figure 9 illustrates the anticipated and unanticipated outcomes of the doctrine during actual implementation.

The commitment of the Highcroft staff to the goal of collaboration in planning programs, solving problems, and celebrating success was clear in the various examples provided in the narrative. Richard supported teacher planning time, encouraged them to engage in team planning, and sought their ideas on such issues as maintaining a sense of balance within an extensive list of responsibilities. From the beginning of planning the school in January 1978, Richard formalized his beliefs about coping with stress through an ad hoc committee he called "the committee to take care of all of us." The stresses in opening any school year are great, but in a new open-space school that relies on collaboration, the stress is compounded. This was certainly the case with the breakdown in third grade. The stress associated with that episode would continue through the end of school and a summer of much-needed recuperation.

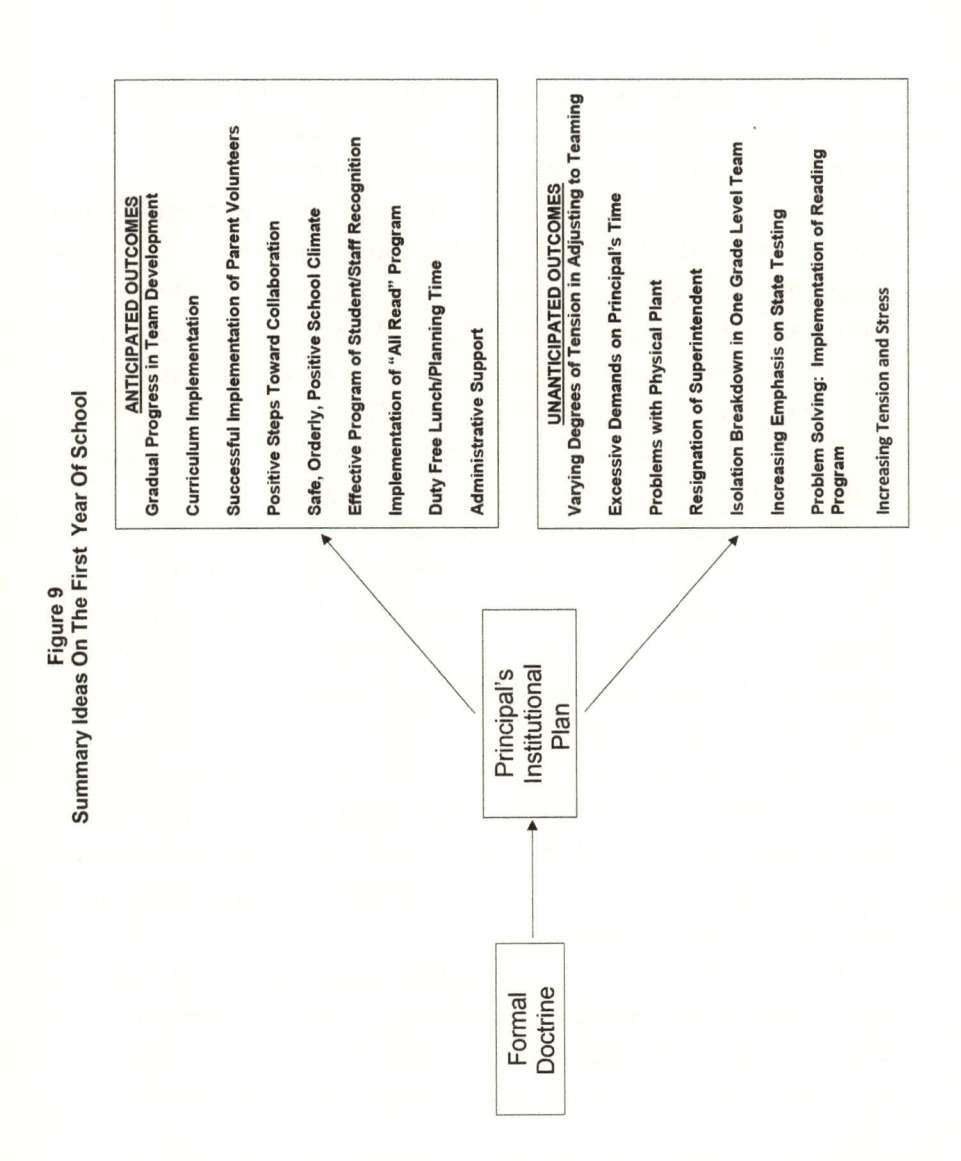

Figure 9
Summary Ideas On The First Year Of School

ANTICIPATED OUTCOMES
- Gradual Progress in Team Development
- Curriculum Implementation
- Successful Implementation of Parent Volunteers
- Positive Steps Toward Collaboration
- Safe, Orderly, Positive School Climate
- Effective Program of Student/Staff Recognition
- Implementation of "All Read" Program
- Duty Free Lunch/Planning Time
- Administrative Support

UNANTICIPATED OUTCOMES
- Varying Degrees of Tension in Adjusting to Teaming
- Excessive Demands on Principal's Time
- Problems with Physical Plant
- Resignation of Superintendent
- Isolation Breakdown in One Grade Level Team
- Increasing Emphasis on State Testing
- Problem Solving: Implementation of Reading Program
- Increasing Tension and Stress

Formal Doctrine → Principal's Institutional Plan → (Anticipated Outcomes, Unanticipated Outcomes)

In June, after school had closed, I interviewed several teachers to understand how they felt about the five months of planning that began in January 1978. One teacher discussed the significance of the initial meeting when they all came together for the first time: "I remember in January when we all first met and everyone introduced themselves, and especially when teachers began discussing their

On Becoming a School Principal

credentials, and my thought was, *My gosh, what am I doing here?* It was a little frightening, you know, and I think that instilled in me that I really needed to do well. I worked my tail off and had a good year."

Another teacher talked about the value of early planning and the impact it had on getting through a busy school year: "I think it [planning meetings] was a good idea because we gelled. I think we were a unit before school even began. We were comfortable with one another when school started. Most of us were relating on a first-name basis. We had a common goal, and Richard set the tone. There was a lot to contend with because the building was not completely done. We learned to be flexible and work together."

Another teacher spoke of advance planning this way: "It prepared me to know what was ahead of us. I felt I really had a stake in the school. After all that planning [January–May], by the beginning of the year, I felt that this is my school. We had been there since the beginning. It wasn't Richard's school; it was our school. Personally, that was important to me."

There is always much to do to get a school ready for children. And even though teachers found the meetings to be tedious at times, they saw the value of early preparation. In view of the accumulated stress during the year, teachers felt the advanced planning helped them achieve a great deal.

Richard's decision to use a temporary system to deal with the mass of operational details also provided a natural means for building a school culture of participative cooperation. Although physically demanding, his plan was an innovative approach to school planning.

CHAPTER 12
Analysis and Implications

Introduction

This study examined the organizational development of a new elementary school with a novel architectural design. The primary goal was to understand the processes and procedures involved in a series of monthly meetings to plan the opening of the school through the first full year of operations. Because the school was to be an open flexible space facility, considerable attention was devoted to the socialization of the staff as a collaborative team. The manner in which teachers achieved cooperative team teaching and the principal's role in the process were of particular interest.

The analysis of findings begins with the principal and his origins during the Great Depression. The earlier narrative provided a window to his early life and circumstances that was influential to his maturation and eventual path as an educator. The planning and implementation of a new open-space school was significant because it implied a change in the way a school was managed. The findings suggest the principal's role was critical in initial efforts to develop a collaborative team.

Collaboration has implications for teachers who are usually on the receiving end of efforts to create change. It was the principal's intention to involve teachers in creating organizational structures that required fresh thinking about their professional work. The underlying structure of grade-level teams deliberating on instructional plans within an open environment, where their teaching skills were visible to others, was a departure from the isolation of traditional schools. This new reality prompted questions regarding how the mix of personalities and professional experience would meld as a team. The principal was a key player in the plan and drew heavily upon his personal philosophy, leadership experience, beliefs and values, and capacity for leading a new organization of immense complexity.

The analysis draws from a number of sources representing current research on educational change, school reform, the professional development of teachers, and the implications for principals who seek school improvement through collaboration. Further, the analysis weaves significant aspects of the earlier narrative into the various points of view drawn from the literature.

Nature or Nurture

A decades-long debate about whether leaders are actually born or are made has produced mixed results. Dozier (2014) and others (Waldman, Bernard, and Walter, 2009; Wagner, 2009; Seltzer and Barnard, 2008) argue that leaders are born with basic leadership skills that are improved through experience and learning opportunities with established leaders. Others (Chen and Bliese 2002) adhere to the position that good leadership is only achievable through trial and error experience. The middle ground position in the debate sidesteps the "chicken or egg" explanation for the simple reality that nature and nurture are both involved in shaping leadership potential.

The circumstances of Richard's birth at the start of the Great Depression imposed wide-ranging survival issues for his family. He witnessed extreme poverty and the significance of a strong work ethic, taking on jobs to help his family maintain essentials for life. His exposure to racial discrimination and disenfranchisement of the poor helped him understand what people were experiencing. His parents modeled humility and determination in the face of desperate economic conditions. These and other related factors within his environment produced a positive sense of whom he was and what he needed to do in order to be successful. He was ambitious, and over time, his ambition was associated with actions that would improve conditions for people.

The progression from boyhood through adolescence followed a process of "differentiation" that Firestone et al. (2013) described as the struggle everyone faces in striving to reach a sense of self as a unique person. The path is marked by pain and rejection from environmental influences and the need to change aversive elements that interfere with reaching the true self. Richard was wholly unprepared to assume teaching at the age of seventeen, but he took advantage of every opportunity to advance himself. Ambition and determination helped to mediate the struggle.

In her book *Leadership in Turbulent Times* (2018), Doris Kearns Goodwin observed that at moments of great challenge, leaders are able to bring forth talents to enlarge the lives and opportunities of others. In citing Lincoln as one example, Goodwin reminds us of his particular ambition, which was in conjunction with his empathic understanding, that always connected to the passions of people he served. She concluded that leaders of towering ego whose ambition is divorced from the best outcomes for people behaved more like despots.

Awakened Leadership

Leadership is often described as a "style," each with its particular character. The list is long, but a few examples include resonant leadership, laissez-faire leadership, charismatic leadership, authentic leadership, and crisis leadership. The list is incomplete because leadership is a dynamic and continuously evolving enterprise. In her intense study of a small sample of people identified as successful leaders, Marques (2009) introduced a variant she described as "awakened leadership," which, according to her analysis, has broader applicability, unlike the majority of styles that relate to one type of leader or one type of situation. To Marques's way of thinking, the awakened leadership style is applicable to a broad array of situations and is characterized as highly flexible. Such an approach to leadership may resonate with new patterns of thinking in a globalized, interconnected world fueled by information.

Marques offers an interesting combination of qualities exhibited by awakened leaders. These include moral and ethical values, integrity, honesty and trust; also important are kindness, forgiveness, courage, love, and deep listening. Awakened leaders are made by life and experience while growing up. Such a leader may have been born with certain skills that enhanced his or her potential, but the "wakefulness" within the leader surfaces through trial and error. This leader approaches all situations in the same manner, whether alone, in a group, addressing a large audience, or among friends: graceful, kind, empathetic, respectful, and down to earth.

Expansion of the Principal's Responsibilities

The role of principal has evolved over the years. As schools gradually expanded from one room to several classrooms, school boards identified a "principal teacher" who took on coordination responsibilities along with teaching children. With consolidation and urbanization, schools became more organized, and the permanent role of principal was institutionalized. As the public clamor for improved achievement occurred, the principal assumed broader duties as instructional leader who worked with teachers on alignment of instruction. Instructional leadership may have been important, but it did not necessarily lead to improved achievement.

However, the principalship has taken on different meanings over the past decades. The principal was often defined as a "gatekeeper" managing the ebb and flow of materials and policies. This minimizes and indeed misses the existing demand for the kind of thinking that builds the professional competence of teachers who have the primary influence on pupil learning. According to Collins (2001), successful leaders seek the timeless search for principles that remain constant, true, and relevant, no matter how the world changes. I would argue that such driving beliefs are critical to principals and teachers who seek to improve schooling.

So what kind of leadership do schools need in order to improve? Where should the discussion begin? Is the principal the key to school reform? Or should teachers be the focus of attention? Perhaps parents and children have an important role in school improvement since they are the primary clients of schooling. Fullan (2016) has examined the issue in great detail, reaching the conclusion that all roles need to be better understood. I will begin the analysis with the principalship.

It is abundantly clear that the role of principal has become increasingly complex. Complexity should be met with technical skills and, perhaps most important, sound human skills. In Collins' 2001 study of high performing leaders (that is, "level five leaders"), he identified certain qualities associated with sustained success over time. The level five leader displays a humble persona and a professional will, along with a quiet intensity and an unwavering capacity to do what had to be done. According to Collins, the level five leader has ambition, but it is channeled away from ego satisfaction to the greater good of the organization.

We often hear leaders say that people are most important, but Collins found that level five leaders believe the "right" people are the most important asset, and the degree of success an organization has depends on finding the right people who are assigned important tasks. In all cases, level five leaders seek simplicity by thinking about the following: what they are passionate about, what they could do better than anyone else, and what drives them to perform. Collins proposes that the intersection of these points produces a personal conception of leadership.

However, the question of complexity in the life of a leader is significant. When dissected, a variety of qualities, skills, or potentials rise to be considered. Jappinen (2014) has described the emergence of human interactional "sensemaking" as part of the complexity of educational leadership. She suggests that many interacting components are present in leadership dialogue—and understanding the complexity of these factors can improve leadership effectiveness. School leaders are confronted by theories, points of view, and politically driven calls for action, and the ability to make sense of the stream of data that requires careful thought.

As an approach to sensemaking, several researchers (Klein, Sayam, Faratin, and Bar-Yam 2003) have suggested interaction and negotiation as prerequisites for understanding the kinds of meanings given to diverse elements of interaction. Weick (2005) has explained how sensemaking deals with interplay between action and interpretation. This is the precise point where complexity resides. In her thesis on "awakened" leaders, Marques highlighted the significance of "deep listening" in trying to make sense of interactions. Given the current state of the principalship, time, ongoing management pressures, and unanticipated distractions are impediments to deep listening, which requires extended uninterrupted time.

The Collaborative School

In a prescient report on the meaning of collaborative school, Smith and Scott (1990) discussed the contrast between traditional and collaborative approaches in managing schools. In short, the long history of teaching in traditional schools is a story about teachers' isolation from each other, with little interaction about how to improve their skills. The principal's contact with teachers is connected to evaluation processes without ongoing feedback about improvement. Faculty members seldom come together to discuss ideas about school improvement. In comparison, teachers in collaborative settings see themselves as working together to improve schooling. A collegial atmosphere encourages teachers to learn from each other through observation and discussion. It is commonplace for teachers in collaborative schools to share effective practices with new colleagues. As Fullan (2018) has so aptly stated, as teachers develop shared meaning and knowledge, they credit the principal who engenders in them and their students a vision for the school's success and provides practical support to their efforts. Most significantly, teachers point to each other as resources for solving problems.

The narrative revealed a pattern of interaction that brought Richard into direct contact with pupils and teachers every day. He was able to assess the pulse of the school through his informal presence. His regular meetings with grade-level teams and meetings to decipher specific issues or problems were substantive and required listening, troubleshooting, negotiations, and solutions. He made time for this type of dialogue, which teachers often initiated individually or as a team. His communications were the foundation of collaboration. The concept of collaborative, as a noun based on agency as "co" and action as "labor," enlightens how collaboration worked at Highcroft. It was a structure featuring interdependent planning and decision-making, and the principal was sometimes directly there and at other times in the background of deliberations as decisions were made.

How do we know that collaboration works? Collaboration is a stark contrast to the isolation of traditional schools. In recent years, education research has produced valuable evidence explaining why some schools become unusually successful. One important study involved the University of Chicago's Consortium on Chicago School Research (Bryk, Sebring, Allensworth, Luppescu, and Easton 2010). Demographic information, test data, and extensive surveys of stakeholders in more than four hundred Chicago elementary schools over a fifteen-year period outlined the kinds of organizational characteristics and practices predictive of above-average improvement in student outcomes. After controlling for demographic factors, the data suggested that the most successful schools had an unusually high degree of trust among their administrators, teachers, and parents.

Five organizational features were connected to this finding:

1. A sensible instructional guidance system, coordinated within and across grade levels, was identified as a strength.
2. Successful schools worked to improve instructional capacity by making it possible for teachers to observe each other, providing ongoing support and opportunities to work with resources outside the school.
3. Strong connections were observed between parents, teachers, volunteers, and others in the community.
4. A student-centered learning climate that responded to individual needs was prominent.

Successful schools cultivated relationships between teachers, parents, and community members who became invested in assisting with school improvement. A hallmark of Richard's leadership was his belief that building trust and positive relationships was essential to a school's success.

Pitfalls in Selection of the Right People

Prior to accepting the principal's position at Highcroft, Richard had some exposure to open-plan schools and alternative teaching methods within flexible space. However, he didn't let his limited experience interfere with plans for Highcroft, an opportunity he had been waiting for all his life. He was on the precipice of an entirely new approach to education, and the long term planning process itself would evolve as a significant innovation. After preparing a written plan of action, his first step was selection of teachers and staff. In considering a vast array of details, this particular step was consequential. Although Collins's 2001 studies were not focused on education, the applications were obvious. According to Collins, the level five leader's first task is hiring the best people available. Collins asserts that the right people are your most important asset.

In the world of business, a leader may have greater latitude in selecting the "right" people. This is not always the case with staffing of schools. For example, a principal may have limited choice due to transfer policies within a school district. When a new school opens, other schools are redistricted and lose students; some teachers have to be moved. Therefore, a principal may not have complete control over hiring. However, Richard was assertive in his teacher selection process and managed to fill teaching positions with people he had worked with or who came highly recommended. He took advantage of interviews, often hours long, to reveal their technical and human strengths. In this regard, his ambition was on full display, not for personal gain or ego but for the school.

However, although hiring practices have become more science based in recent years, it is still a human enterprise and, as such, is far from perfect. At Highcroft, Richard was fortunate to have direct knowledge of key people who served as leaders at each grade level. Some of these teachers had worked with him at previous schools, and he was familiar with their strong human skills. Others, although less well known, were nonetheless highly recommended by teachers or others he trusted. A few were transfers he had to accept. A mixed set of circumstances determined the Highcroft staff.

Collins (2001) spoke about the importance of vetting in finding the right people. But he also advocated that when there are doubts, don't hire. Richard understood the imperfections of staff selection and the possibility that mistakes might be made. In such situations, Collins reiterated his view that a leader must be rigorous rather than ruthless and must act when a change in people is required. Ultimately, when he knew the system of collaboration was in jeopardy at one grade level, Richard utilized the staff evaluation policy to make a change. He experienced significant stress in taking this course of action.

Once the staff had been selected and the series of monthly planning meetings began, staff members described Richard as "demanding and giving" in conducting his duties. He had a consistency of style and often demonstrated his sense of humor as work continued. As the machinery of organization was established, Richard and teachers began work as a team in addressing all needs. At times, grade-level teams met on their own to plan curricula, and nearly everyone volunteered for ad hoc work groups to deal with unique needs. Richard's approach was similar to Collins's stance on leadership: leadership was rigorous, but not ruthless, and driven by an unwavering drive to achieve important ends.

Perhaps the best descriptor of this process is what Collins (2001) refers to as the "flywheel concept." In earlier times, the flywheel was an important tool. Imagine a huge steel wheel with belts that connected it to smaller wheels and axels that interact in ways to accomplish work, such as grinding seeds into flour or producing movement in other machines. Nothing can be accomplished until the flywheel begins to move, and energy must initially be applied to help it gain momentum. It may require a push for several revolutions, but at some point, it takes off on its own. Richard introduced ideas, techniques, general and specific goals; and he continued to input energy until individuals and small groups of teachers were actively involved. Collins (2001) would say that results come from a series of good decisions (that is, several turns of the wheel) diligently implemented one after another.

Richard possessed deep beliefs about the nature of a school. He had a quiet fanaticism about the essential concept of school as a culture of disciplined people who maintained their focus on elements they agreed upon as important. However, outside intrusions, such as the newest strategy or technique reported in the literature, can be a distraction to established plans. Richard adopted what Collins (2001) called "rinsing the cottage cheese" to remove the fat as a means of dealing with unimportant ideas. In schooling terms, it could be construed as maintaining faith and effort in what you do best and eliminate, or at least reduce, peripheral issues and distractions. In Collins's view, ideas such as discipline, rigor, diligence, precision, methodicalness, and focus were essential after everything else was "rinsed out."

During teacher interviews, Richard explained the kind of school he thought Highcroft would become. Then, when he met teachers at the first meeting in January 1978, he reiterated his beliefs about children—their individual differences and needs. He emphasized the expectation that teachers would be instrumental in planning a collaborative school. At that moment in time, teachers were active in their willingness to engage in the process, and the narrative suggested strong interest in working with others to develop plans. The mechanism for actualizing these outcomes was the planning process itself. There were no separate workshops to develop interpersonal skills, communications, or the development of a positive school climate.

Richard had placed considerable emphasis on selecting teachers who were good persons, and he was diligent in identifying teachers with empathy, caring, listening, patience, and kindness. These factors were the superstructure for collaboration at Highcroft. Therefore, the "temporary system" (Miles 1964) of long-term planning became the training modality for building collaboration.

Professional Development of Teachers

In 1978, the idea of professional development of teachers was common in conversations among educators, but the profession languished in the traditional system of teacher isolation. Workshops, seminars, and university courses were typical modes for the continuing education of teachers. However, the content of these venues did not automatically translate to changes in instructional practices (Fullan 2018). Teachers still largely worked in isolation with little ongoing substantive contact with colleagues. Individual teacher characteristics and historical predispositions about personal growth contributed to the stalemate. In addition, a teacher's psychological state may influence the degree of openness to new ideas. Fullan stated that teachers—depending on personality, experience, and stage of career—might vary in their degree of self-actualization and sense of efficacy, both of which are connected to taking persistent action when implementing instructional techniques. In short, the teaching profession has lacked a technical culture and the development of a shared language, which, when actively used, is, according to Fullan, a predictor of success as teachers and principals work together to improve schools.

So assuming that these points are accurate, how should educators proceed? Which constructions can ultimately lead to actions that shared meaning, a technical culture, and a common language? Beabout (2012) has suggested that learning through interaction is the singular element in understanding educational complexity. Interaction leads to clarification of one's point of view, allows for questions, and fleshes out details, all of which help to build a common language. Senge (1990) and others (Bandura 1997; Gronn, 2002, 2008; Harris, 2009; MacBeath 2005) argue that interaction among teachers is fundamental to developing a learning organization, and the distribution of leadership among participants promotes teacher efficacy. Dufour (2004), Fullan (2006), and Hargreaves and Fink (2006) believe leadership should be a matter of importance to everyone in an educational community and is essential to development of a collaborative culture.

One of the most promising ideas regarding professionalization of teachers is building their capacity for helping to create change.

A report titled "Teacher-Initiated Projects: Strengthening the Role of the Teacher as a Participant in Educational Change" (Mosher 1984) presented case study findings of teachers who received small grants from a teacher center to develop educational projects. The projects involved one teacher, a small group, or even an entire school and covered curricular innovations, group process skills, and action research. This program was eventually adopted by the Missouri Department of Elementary and secondary education, providing extended opportunities for teacher-designed programs, but unfortunately it was discontinued due to funding constraints. However, the study indicated positive results at several levels: personal, professional, and institutional. The report cited the value of grassroots program development as a means of expanding and extending professional capacity.

Educational Change

In a large sense, Highcroft was a planned departure from the traditional form of school organization. Historically, the traditional school consisted of individual classrooms led by a teacher in charge of large group instruction that relied heavily on lecture, seatwork, and recitation. A principal who made decisions about scheduling and allocating resources managed the school. Teachers were isolated from colleagues, and there was little time for substantive interaction about professional work. In comparison, Highcroft was arranged as open grade-level pods with flexible walls that allowed an array of activities planned by teaching teams. Thus the structure of Highcroft was a change in the traditional approach to teaching. Miles (1964) defined "change" as an alteration in goals, structure, or processes of a system as observed between distinct points in time.

Within this scenario, a question arises regarding whether Highcroft was also an innovation, defined as a "deliberate, novel, specific change, thought to be more efficacious in accomplishing the goals of a system" (Miles 1964: 14). Highcroft was innovative in the sense that architecture was designed to support teacher collaboration in planning instruction. Further, management of a collaborative school was also innovative because leadership was distributed beyond the typical control of one person, the principal. So at the outset of planning, Highcroft would initiate a new form of decentralized decision-making that stood in stark contrast to other schools of the time.

After years of studying schools and the change process, Fullan (2018) proposed a definition that reflects the shifting emphasis in the teacher's role and responsibilities. He argues that a well-founded change processes shapes and reshapes good ideas as it simultaneously builds capacity and ownership among the users of the change. This conception is accompanied by a prediction that posits if either component is missing, the change will likely fail.

As Richard began to work with Highcroft teachers in January 1978, he never discussed the formal aspects of "change" or "innovation," but he presented an ambitious set of beliefs and goals related to the importance of education in the present and future, in addition to the significance of personal human qualities modeled by teachers. That was the grand structure upon which the Highcroft culture was to be constructed. The care and treatment of people was the point of the spear, and the solid application of good teaching followed. In Fullan's thinking, these were the "drivers" of the change they hoped to implement. The "right drivers" are capacity builders for everything the school would do: solid results in learning, collaborative work, reliance on pedagogy. It was a knitted system.

Educational Change: An Imperfect Process

Change is common in education, is often exciting, and is frequently confronted by factors that have not been thoroughly considered, especially those experienced at a personal level. Sometimes the speed at which change occurs makes it difficult for individuals to consider the implications. As a prelude to deeper thought about the change process at Highcroft, it may be useful to review specific elements that determine the success or failure of a change effort.

It should be readily apparent that changes in educational systems involve people who react to new experiences initially through a familiar, reliable visualization of reality (Fullan 2018). People tend to attach personal meaning to the elements of a change, regardless of how meaningful it may be to others. According to Fullan, participants in the change process tend to think about change through the possession of their own experience, which in turn provides the assurance for mastering something new. Change may be imposed or voluntarily initiated because the outcome offers the opportunity to expand professional skills and build personal capacity. However, whatever the change may entail, it may not be immediately clear to participants who may be ambivalent about the proposed change. Thus ambivalence cannot be overcome until the "meaning" of the change is understood.

Fullan has been thinking about educational change in all its manifestations since 1972, when he published a paper titled "Overview of the Innovative Process and the User." In his language, "user" refers to people who become engaged with a change and put it into practice. He concluded that this approach led to no significant change at the level of the user. Hence, if a change is to be successfully implemented, it must involve teachers in the meaning of the innovation and allow opportunities to help shape it.

Through a temporary system of extensive planning, Richard and teachers steadily advanced the understanding of requirements for successful teaching in an open-concept school where team planning is essential to decision-making. Cooperative work was omnipresent in all planning activities. In considering decisions about teaching practices, individual teachers followed a scheme that is typical in confronting change; they were compelled to measure proposed changes against the ways they would need to adapt their approach to teaching. This is so, according to Fullan, because teachers do not immediately understand the expectations and ramifications of change. Teachers are not immediately aware of all the dimensions underlying teamwork, and working through the unknowns is an essential part of the process of initiating change.

John Dewey (1916) was known for his philosophy of learning by doing. In delving deeper into Dewey's views, Fullan (2018) explained a deeper intent. According to Fullan, Dewey believed that people do not learn by doing per se but by thinking about what they plan to do. Fullan suggests that the stimulation that attends new experiences exposes new ideas that stimulate thinking among teachers who have the primary responsibility for implementing any change in practice. If leaders don't engage teachers through partnerships and collaborative cultures, the probability for success is remote. Barth (1990) has argued that shared leadership is a promising solution for energizing school reform and improvement. The principal's role is instrumental in empowering teachers as leaders in assuming responsibility for the well-being of a school. When shared leadership engages staff, parents, and students, a synergy of action can result in the improvement of schools and pupil achievement.

I assert that when a collaborative culture is comprehensive in building leadership skills for a professional learning community, it will eventually profit all who have interests in developing effective schools, including principals, teachers, and especially students. Finally, the research shows that learning in a social context is deeper than independent learning through typical devices such as workshop and conference attendance. Thus collaborative work may be a more effective approach to professional development of teachers.

Implications for the Future

The narrative attempted to describe several aspects of a principal's growth as a leader and his responsibilities for planning the opening of a novel open-plan school, based on a collaborative model of organization. The implications that follow are assertions derived from my own proximity to the data and examples from the literature. Perhaps other implications may be drawn, and in the spirit of participant observation research, readers are encouraged to draw their own implications and conclusions.

- I argue that principals who lead collaborative schools should possess the skills of "awakened leaders" who possess self-understanding, a capacity for deep listening, and a wide range of genuine interpersonal skills. A thorough grounding in building relationships and trust is paramount.
- Elementary school principals who devote time to the complexities of a school culture should have the assistance of others who can deflect the constant flow of problems and issues that demand attention. Leading a collaborative school is intense, and a principal's primary focus of attention should be on teacher interactions, implementation of curricula, promoting teacher leadership, and engaging the community.
- Teachers in a collaborative school should receive exposure to the benefits and pitfalls of team planning and teaching prior to implementation. The commitment to teamwork and group decision-making may be accompanied by excitement, a willingness to learn and adapt, and the ability to set aside personal preferences for better ideas from team members, which may mask latent impediments to effective group process. A wise principal should be aware of early signs of group dysfunction and provide assistance when required
- At Highcroft, Richard made a commitment to teachers for team planning time and a duty-free lunch. A principal assigned to implement a collaborative school should be aware of the time demands of teachers and take steps to ensure that adequate planning time is provided in the schedule.

EPILOGUE

Introduction

In 1984, I returned to Highcroft for a five-year follow-up to the 1978 study. There were several underlying goals involved. In a general sense, I wanted to see how the school was doing now at age five. I was curious about what, if anything, had changed. In the midst of the earlier study, there was no practical way to consider "sustainability" or long-term success of programs and practices Of course, I was curious about open space and how teachers had acclimated to team planning and teaching in classrooms without walls. The methods of study were the same: qualitative inquiry through the strategy of participant observation. I began the work in November 1984 and concluded in February 1985. While I was not present every day, I managed to spend time each week observing within the school and classrooms. Observations were recorded in field notes, and formal and informal interviews were conducted with Richard, teachers, and staff similar to the original study in 1978. The findings are reported below.

Initial Impressions

I had not visited Highcroft since I'd concluded the research in 1979. My initial plan was to do a brief follow-up study five years later, and it began in November 1984, when I attended an early morning staff meeting. Prior to the meeting, I took a few minutes to reacquaint myself with the building. The interior was much the same as in 1978: soft colors, low tables with lamps along hallways, antique furniture and other items scattered about, and lots of colorful student artwork on walls everywhere in the school. As in 1978, you couldn't escape the feeling that this was someone's home, an aesthetically warm and secure place, a special place for children to learn.

However, there was one new addition: a front porch with a swing. In the space between the entrance to the main office and the nurse's office, Richard, with the help of his wife, had constructed the edifice consisting of two upright posts, a slanted roof with cedar shingles, and a porch railing between the two front posts. On the blank wall behind the swing, Myra used art materials to create a large window that gave the appearance of a view inside the house. Porches with swings were common in country homes in and around Duncans Bridge, and Richard's porch was another cherished connection to a way of life long past.

Children who waited for their parents sat in the swing. Richard met with children who were receiving happy grams or rose recognition as they sat with him on the swing. He celebrated student birthdays there, and sometimes he sat by himself, speaking to children and teachers as they passed. The porch and other decor were visible reminders of the informality that existed in working relationships among adults and children at Highcroft.

Aside from the decor, there were also several organizational and programmatic changes. The first was the school district decision to join the St. Louis Voluntary Desegregation Program (more commonly called the VTS or Voluntary Transfer System), which resulted in forty-five African American children being transferred to Highcroft in 1980. Because of the school district's decision to join the VTS, alterations in curriculum and organization were required to meet their unique needs for learning, including counseling, home and school communications and individualized support.

Highcroft soon became aware that parents of VTS children did not attend parent conferences, and Richard and teachers responded by meeting parents at a community college near their homes. Richard identified a Highcroft staff member as a liaison to parents from the city to provide clear access to teachers.

Another significant change involved the proposed adoption of a middle school program that would eventually affect the organization of both elementary and high schools. Although not yet implemented, elementary schools would lose the sixth grade, leading to changes in teaching staff and curriculum organization. Together these changes also influenced the planned construction of additional classroom space on the west end of Highcroft to accommodate additional VTS students.

In 1980, a new superintendent replaced a long-standing superintendent who had been responsible for the construction of several open-space schools during his tenure. The new superintendent had an agenda with far-reaching implications for schools and school leaders in the school district.

Staff Meeting

The meeting began at 7:50 a.m. in the music room, with forty-four teachers and staff arranged in a circle around the room. Since 1978, the method of recognizing staff, commonly called the "Rose Program," had been formalized by the addition of a rose rug that had been placed in the center of the room for a ceremony later in the meeting. As I looked around the room, I saw familiar faces, but there were many I didn't know. Of the forty-four certificated staff present, sixteen, or approximately 36 percent, were new to Highcroft since 1978. The agenda followed a familiar pattern of announcements, comments from teachers about a recently completed staff retreat, and drawings for door prizes, always enjoyed by everyone. This could easily have been recognized as a staff meeting in 1978: informal, openness to anyone who wanted to speak, a high degree of familiarity, ease of discussion, and outright fun.

The meeting closed with the rose recognition of sixth-grade teachers who came forward and either kneeled or sat on the rug while Richard complimented them for their exceptional work. There were many smiles around the room and everyone was attentive to Richard's words. This was yet another reminder of recognition and celebration as a norm of Highcroft.

Creative Teaching, Staffing, and Collaborative Planning in Open Space

The earlier narrative described Richard's approach to staff selection in 1978. He hired some teachers with whom he had prior experience. He listened to recommendations from teachers he trusted and conducted lengthy interviews with all potential candidates. He was compelled to work with the district teacher transfer policy that interfered with his selection process. In addition, in every aspect of identifying prospective teachers, he searched diligently for good persons, teachers who demonstrated excellent human skills.

Due to a reduction in force (RIF) policy imposed by the district in the school year 1979–1980, he was prevented from hiring teachers from the outside. He spoke of a "district pool" of teachers in filling vacancies. During that period, Richard described how teachers who knew they were leaving waited until the last minute to resign in order to avoid putting Richard in the position of selecting someone from the bottom of the barrel. In discussing that period, Richard spoke of staff loyalty to the school and the desire to maintain the quality of collaboration in grade-level teams. Although it was not allowed by the transfer policy during RIF, Richard "recruited" teachers quietly behind the scenes to position Highcroft as a school that a teacher would want to join. Highcroft teachers were also active in identifying teachers thought to be a good fit for the Highcroft school culture. It suggested that teachers understood the importance of the right people in carrying forward the goals of the school. Richard was aware of the risks involved in this clandestine approach to staffing, but he was not deterred.

The manner in which teachers conducted their work team planning was open for all to see, just as it was in 1978, when school opened. However, I couldn't help but notice the ease of their interactions with pupils and each other. The urgency of implementing the programs and routines of a new school, originally so apparent in 1978, had given way to an atmosphere of familiarity and comfort with their roles and responsibilities. Teachers had given a great deal of attention to the creation of novel activities that included instructional displays on bulletin boards and walls within class areas.

I arrived early on November 18 and observed children entering the building, talking quietly as they moved purposefully to their class areas. I was observing the children entering the third-grade pod, where they were greeted by a teacher who discussed materials and games they might need. The students began working individually, in pairs, and in small groups on puzzles, math problems, and language arts materials. The teacher described the scene as a "great anticipatory set for the entire day." There were plenty of examples of this pattern across all grade levels. The presence of teachers could be noted everywhere before the actual start of school, but formal hallway supervision had been replaced by informal work with children before the day began.

One third grader told me about the two antique desks off to the side. She described them as the "spotlight desks," a place of special recognition for a pupil's accomplishment. She went on to say, "If you are picked to sit there, you can ask a friend to sit in the other desk." You couldn't miss the importance she attached to receiving this honor.

All the class areas in the building were incredibly rich in colorful objects, bulletin boards with aesthetic and instructional things, and materials of all kinds. Just by being there, you couldn't avoid the feeling of stimulation. One would conclude that the way teachers had tended to these details suggested that the entire school was a special place for learning.

A second-grade teacher was leading children in singing the school song, "Up, Up with Highcroft," and one student waited at the door until they were done. The teacher brought it to the attention of the class. "Boys and girls, did you notice that Sally waited at the door until we finished? That was a very grown-up thing to do." Timely recognition such as this was common in 1978 and, along with rose recognition and happy grams, helped to maintain a positive and respectful atmosphere. The emphasis on student and staff recognition continued in 1984.

Enter the New Superintendent

The new superintendent was considerably different in temperament and philosophy compared to his predecessor. His tenure began quietly enough in 1980 as he visited schools to get acquainted. Every superintendent has an agenda of his own or "marching orders" from the board of education. One of his goals, among others, was his intent to move principals to break up sectors of power that developed in previous years. It wasn't immediately clear just how it would work, but principals began to speculate. For example, who would be moved and why? Would effective principals be transferred to ineffective schools? Similarly, would a principal deemed ineffective be moved to an effective school. These were unknown aspects of the transfer plan.

When the smoke cleared, so did the mystery about the initiation of the policy. It began with the transfer of some of the secondary administrators and then moved to elementary principals. Some of the elementary principals volunteered to be moved and felt fortunate to be moved to schools that were performing well. Most liked the idea of being transferred and welcomed it. However, not all were as accepting, including Richard, but he suspected that he would be forced to move and was adamant in his unwillingness to participate.

As a group, elementary principals were concerned about priorities for action and funding by the board of education. The superintendent had other priorities, and a conflict began to emerge. All elementary schools in the district had part-time nurses. Principals believed that changing conditions (VTS Program) in the needs of students required not only full-time nurses but also additional counseling and reading assistance. These factors led to consideration of how to address their concerns. In Richard's case, he began discussing needs and concerns with the executive committee of his parent-teacher organization. During a meeting in November 1984, Richard began to create awareness:

> We talked last time about some things to get going on. The district isn't like it was. It's different now with the voluntary desegregation program. The kids are not going to be as well prepared. We are dealing with kids from parents going through a divorce. The conditions [affecting schools] are different ... Because of changing conditions, our counselor is overloaded. We now have two and a half times the number of children with reading problems than we did in nineteen seventy-eight. The addition of forty-five kids from the city has impacted us. We are scheduled to have one hundred. It is time that we move politically to get the staff increased. I've never said that to you before, have I?

The response: "No, it's going to have to come from you."

The VTS represented a significant change, and principals were trying to cope with the needs of children who were transferred. Parents of these children were not likely to come to school for conferences and, at least at Highcroft, Richard and teachers arranged to meet with city parents in their neighborhood. He also identified a staff member to serve as a liaison to parents of VTS children, which provided a clear connection to Highcroft teachers.

Additional societal changes were also growing in prominence. The clamor for large-scale testing was oppressive, and most schools recoiled from calls for action from pundits, the state legislature, the state department of education, and the United States Department of Education. Those who expressed reservations about the impact it would have on teachers and schools were not heard. Schools were also reacting to changes in family structure and the tendency to have schools provide before and after school supervision for children from homes with one parent or where both parents worked. The school district responded by sponsoring latchkey programs that met an immediate need but did not consider how it would affect school facilities and staffing. Richard commented about it during the meeting of the PSO [Parent School Organization]:

> There is a growing concern across the country about the number of children who go to day care centers. A latchkey program has been started by the YMCA [in the school district]. I am against that for this school. It is bad for a principal to say something negative about a program for kids. It's just one more thing we have to do in a school.

He spoke further about schools becoming the remedy for societal problems as well as the increasing number of add-on programs that require staffing and space but don't receive sufficient funding. Since 1978, the needs of gifted students and computer education were also vying for attention as district-sponsored programs.

Within this scenario of societal forces and calls for schools to do more, we should pause and reflect on Richard's journey from a one-room country school, where math, reading, and social studies were the primary instructional focus. To a certain degree, country schools were regulated by the planting of crops in the spring and the harvest in the fall, when there was a pause in the schedule so children could assist with work on the farm. However, citizens depended upon country schools to provide the basic tools required to function effectively in a democratic society. Children walked, rode a horse or mule, or rode in a wagon to school, and they took pleasure in raising the flag and saying the Pledge of Allegiance each day. Children didn't normally stay after school waiting to be picked up, for they were needed at home. The simplicity of that period and the closeness of teachers, children, and community was part of the background of Richard's beliefs about developing good persons who also could function well in the world.

By 1980, Richard had been either a principal or teacher for thirty-four years and was fifty-one years old. Gifted programs were an unusual innovation that he never had to contend with as an official program. Similarly, he never owned a computer, much less knew how to use one, and the growth of these programs, as well as others previously discussed, were distractions to his belief that schools primarily existed to develop good persons. This was his core belief about schooling. Some might say his beliefs and values were anachronistic or out of touch; neither would be fair in describing Richard's motivation.

During the PSO meeting, one parent made a comment that underscored a dilemma in societal change and the role of public schools in providing support: "But there are single parents. What are they supposed to do?"

Richard replied, "Yes, I agree. If we had space and staff, it would be fine. I think it's inevitable.

Richard followed with a prediction on how the district plan would evolve: "The district will get weaker principals to go with it first. Then the 'middle of the roaders' and finally the holdouts in five years."

Richard would be one of the holdouts. He believed the problem with adding programs was not a matter of money but a disparity in priorities held by district administrators and school principals. In hierarchical systems of management, decisions are often dependent on influence, power, and politics. As a principal, Richard did not like politics and viewed himself as nonpolitical. He held a simple belief: children should be the focus of setting priorities and making decisions about what goes on in schools. He did not want to be a player in this political scheme, but his attitude would soon change.

I recalled an informal meeting with Richard in the fall of 1978, when we discussed staff recognition. I was aware of his intention to invite groups of district employees to lunch at Highcroft to recognize them for their contributions to the opening of Highcroft. The initial group consisted of secretaries in the district office, including the person who worked the switchboard. His plan included maintenance workers, bus drivers, and others. I asked him if there were political motives behind his plan. It was indeed a very ambitious plan, uncommon in most school districts. He said he was motivated by a need to thank people who made direct and indirect contributions to the opening of Highcroft, and he wanted them to feel appreciated. I recall probing further, questioning his motivation. He looked down, and after a few moments of thought, Richard acknowledged that in a small way, politics might be involved, but it wasn't the main reason for his actions.

That was the only time Richard ever spoke of politics as an element of his role as principal. He always spoke of his actions as being helpful to developing good persons. However, in 1980, with a new superintendent in charge of district planning, it was a different set of circumstances that brought Richard's political acumen into full view.

As the meeting of the Highcroft Executive Committee continued, the chairperson initiated discussion about what needed to be done. After much consideration, they decided to address the needs for a full-time nurse. Most of the parents felt it was unacceptable that schools only had part-time nurses. It became a priority for action. They began considering various district groups that should also be engaged in these issues. A citizens advisory council held a phone-in time for people to air concerns. Some mothers held the opinion that it was a weak option. Another parent argued for a steering committee with representation from all schools. The chairperson then stepped in:

Chair: "All PSO presidents have been together, and we are appalled that schools do not have full-time nurses."

Parent number one: "Many principals are reticent to get involved because they feel they can't win."

Parent number two: "But why does it have to involve principals? Why can't we get gobs of people there?"

Parent number three: "To get nurses in every school, it would cost one hundred twenty thousand dollars. If a principal tells his PSO president not to get involved, they won't. We have the largest PSO system of any school in the district. There have been efforts to write letters, make calls, and send mass information to the board of education in the past—and it didn't do any good."

Richard: "You need to know that we are going beyond a full-time nurse to a counselor and more reading help. This school has the same counseling staff and custodians as a school of three hundred."

Parent: "It's a hard year to expect too much from the new superintendent."

Richard: "Yes, you're right. It's going to take more than us. But we have a start. We haven't talked about these things before, have we? It's very risky for a principal to do this. We're supposed to tell you things are wonderful. But there—it's out!"

As parents moved slowly toward developing a plan of action, Richard developed a document titled "It's Elementary, My Dear Watson!" It took the form of a booklet of eight pages intended as a primer for those interested in addressing the issues of staffing. A hand-drawn picture of a little girl dressed in a Sherlock Holmes outfit, smiling and looking through a large magnifying glass, was on the cover. There was a simple introduction on page 1: "Because we care about kids in the district, we feel the time has come to focus on the needs of the elementary school." The contents served as a guide for concerted action by individuals or groups.

Some of the goals were listed on the first page: establish support groups to influence the district, lobby for equity for elementary schools, have enumeration of the staffing needs, and address the needs of elementary children. Other pages provided additional information and guidance on how the plan was to be used. Sample letters to board of education members were included, along with a sample statement for those who chose to make calls to register their concerns. The last page showed how funds could be diverted from the proposed district budget and, if followed, $500,000 could be made available to elementary schools.

Richard shared the booklet with the other elementary principals who were not enthusiastic. Most didn't use it. Highcroft parents and teachers, along with a few brave colleagues, were supportive. However, in the larger cadre of school principals, he was on his own. Richard was a man who cared deeply about children and schools. When he believed he was right, especially regarding what was best for children, he was a force to be reckoned with. To Richard, "speaking truth to power" was a badge of honor.

The superintendent was aware of the clamor about full-time nurses in the elementary schools and vaguely aware that a plan had been formulated. Nevertheless, he was gobsmacked by the vocalization among some elementary principals who supported the idea and called them all to a meeting to discuss the matter. According to four principals in attendance, the superintendent told the group that if no one liked being a principal in the district, he wanted them to leave. One of the elementary principals raised the issue about full-time nurses, and according to those present, the superintendent responded by saying, "You can have an MD in every school, but how are you going to pay for it?"

Richard had been silent until that point, but he responded, saying,

"You can start by eliminating the eight new district administrators you brought with you." Silence enveloped the room!

The superintendent paused, appeared agitated, and expressed his displeasure through a string of expletives directed at Richard. Richard, convinced that his remarks were justified, returned a similar set of expletives to the superintendent. Everyone in the room was quiet, and the meeting came to an abrupt end.

As the principals left, Richard was approached by colleagues who did not outwardly support Richard's plan but complimented him for taking a stand. Others said they admired him for speaking up but admitted they couldn't do it themselves.

Richard told them, "Yes, you can. Just take a magic marker and write 'I agree with Richard' on the palm of your hand, and then just look at it and say it out loud." On the surface, his comment seems facetious, but it was Richard's way of expressing his disapproval of their silence. However, on another level, he understood. He acknowledged that some were young, new to administration, and were frightened of possible retribution. Richard expected retribution. He knew he was one of the principals the superintendent intended to transfer, and that in so doing, Richard might decide to resign. The superintendent didn't know that Richard was no dilettante and, considering his folksy style, certainly wasn't a rube to be trifled with.

Eventually, the PTO Executive Committee became very active in seeking resolution to the staffing issues at Highcroft. Parents believed Highcroft to be an excellent school, and they supported Richard.

One additional outcome was the election of a Highcroft parent to the board of education. Full-time nurses finally became a reality, but discussions on other staffing needs moved slowly. Richard was not entirely aware that a segment of his parents supported gifted education, computer instruction, and latchkey programs at Highcroft. With regard to these programs, Richard could be described as old school. His path to teaching and educational leadership did not resonate with these particular parent interests. However, Richard came to understand the political interests of these parents and eventually became more open to their ideas. However, he was reticent to include these new ideas in his philosophical framework.

In January 1985, I met with the superintendent to discuss my research at Highcroft and my intention to write a book about the school from its inception in 1978. When I asked him for his perceptions of the school, his responses were generally positive, but he voiced concerns about Richard's leadership behavior. He stated that he didn't like the hugging that went on at the school; he was not approving of Richard's practice of hugging teachers and children. Although he didn't cite any specific improprieties, he believed Richard had crossed the line of appropriateness in doing so. I left the interview wondering how the disparity between the points of view of these men was going to work out.

I concluded my follow-up research at Highcroft in February 1985, but later that summer, Richard and I got together. I was curious if the superintendent had transferred him to another school as well as other issues of interest. Richard explained what happened earlier that summer when the superintendent called him. Richard owned a farm and every summer worked in the wheat harvest by driving loads of grain to the storage elevator in nearby Clarence, Missouri. Richard described what happened:

> This summer, I was helping with the harvest on the farm. I was in line at the grain elevator to unload wheat when he [superintendent] called me to tell me he was going to transfer me. So I asked him if he had ever seen someone thrown out of a tavern. He said no. I said, "Well, he grabs hold of a chair, then a table, and when he is moved closer to the door, he grabs the doorjamb with both hands! It's pretty hard to throw a man out when he doesn't want to go."

The superintendent abruptly ended the conversation. Richard was never transferred and remained at Highcroft until he retired on his own terms in 1992.

Sustainability

The first year of Highcroft Ridge Elementary School was a mixture of successes and simmering issues that produced visible changes in Richard's usual ebullient leadership persona. The stress and tension he felt sometimes caused depressed moods, and he was not as accessible to teachers. The staff gradually understood the insurmountable problems among the third-grade team and felt bad for all concerned. However, due to teamwork and collaboration, the staff did not take sides, and continued to function effectively. It was testimony of the degree collaboration that had matured from the initial planning session through the end of the school year.

Fullan (2018) and Collins (2001) each in his own way pointed out that organizational success can't be assessed by examining one year of activity. The question they posed concerned whether the cherished goals of the organization were achieved over time. At Highcroft, the goal of team planning and collaboration was largely successful with the exception of third grade where the breakdown of team planning and teaching was minimal.

During the follow-up study in 1984, the level of collaboration across grade levels was evident in grade-level planning and cooperative decision-making as a school. Thinking back to 1978 and interviews with teachers and then, in January 1978, when the planning sessions began, Richard repeatedly told staff, "In three or four years, Highcroft will be the best elementary school in the district, state, and nation." Teachers were mostly astounded by the immensity of this goal. However, in 1985, Highcroft was recognized as a Gold Star School in Missouri and received the National Excellence in Education Award. *The History of Highcroft* book, maintained religiously by the faculty, captured the moment as follows:

It was the year that the school set out on a deliberate course to be "the best school in the world" became a reality at least in the United States. When it was recognized as a Gold Star School in the state of Missouri and chosen to receive the National Excellence in Education Award from the United States Department of Education. Upon receiving these notifications Richard's antique school bell rang long and loud at Highcroft to let everyone know about the good news.

Richard and a team of teachers went to Washington, DC, to receive the award, and Richard stood with tears in his eyes as the president commended schools receiving the award. Many visitors came to Highcroft to offer congratulations. The list included local officials, two United States senators, and Governor John Ashcroft, who was surprised when he was called to the rose rug to be recognized. It was interesting to watch Richard direct the governor to sit on the rose rug, which he did with a smile. Richard, amid a small audience, followed the Highcroft pattern of reciting the good things for which the governor was recognized.

It seemed clear that Highcroft was sustainable in maintaining its beliefs and goals over the course of five years. One couldn't help but consider that it was the actualization of a self-fulling prophecy.

Following Richard's retirement in 1993, a staff member who had been serving as his assistant replaced him. Her tenure maintained the beliefs and values that formed the Highcroft core since its inception in 1978. When she retired in 2002, she was replaced by a principal who was relatively new to the Highcroft staff and sought to change existing practices. Teachers filled the gap and continued to maintain Highcroft as a collaborative school.

However, with teacher retirements, things began to change, beginning with the removal of the porch, antique memorabilia, and the barnwood wainscot in the teachers' lunch area, installed by Richard and staff members years earlier. One evening Richard and a few helpers went to the school and removed the porch swing and other attributes he and Myra had originally introduced. These alterations changed both the appearance and character of the school. Sadly, it marked the end of a unique system of participation and collaboration. Eventually, all open areas were closed in with walls, and self-contained classrooms became the mode of teaching and learning. It was reminiscent of an observation Sarason (1982) recorded in his book *The Culture of the School and the Problem of Change.* "The more things change, the more they remain the same."

Professional Development and Teaching the "Good Person Ethic"

Richard's work experience had deep roots in the Depression, when work was essential for survival. He worked on the farm, helped with the harvest, learned to pump gas, and delivered groceries to rural people around Duncans Bridge. When he and Myra married, they worked as a team during the summer, painting houses. Richard also did home repairs and small construction projects for local people. The work they did helped to offset the low pay teachers received at the time. Work was second nature to Richard Overfelt.

When children came along, Myra became a stay-at-home mom, and Richard was the primary source of income for the family. In 1972, Richard began teaching education courses through the Extension Division of Northeast Missouri State University and Lincoln University. Extension courses were popular with teachers in meeting certification requirements and advancing themselves on the salary schedule. Adjunct professors were drawn from local school systems and possessed knowledge and skill in teaching adults.

By 1972, Richard had earned BS, MA, and PhD degrees and had completed twenty-six years of education experience in school organization and management. His courses emphasized teacher involvement in a range of subject matter that stressed activities with immediate applications to classrooms. Over his forty-eight years of adult teaching, an estimated five-thousand-plus teachers had enrolled in his courses. It is interesting to note that when the university eventually eliminated the extension division program, they continued to sponsor Richard's courses because of the interest expressed by local teachers. However, at age ninety-one, Richard finally ended his adjunct work in July 2020. The university recognized his years of service with special memorabilia of his contributions, including a formal letter of recognition from the university president.

The typical style of instruction in most extension courses was largely the lecture method, which stood in stark contrast to Richard's approach: direct involvement of his students in creating materials they could use with pupils. This does not mean that his courses lacked substance. The Overfelt curriculum addressed timely themes like managing pupil behavior, learning styles, brain research, and developing a positive classroom atmosphere. The difference was that teachers worked in pairs and small groups to design activities and techniques to engage students. They could be immediately implemented with their students. Activities aimed at developing kindness, respect, caring and support permeated their work.

The narrative previously described the emphasis Richard placed on children as the focus of all instructional planning. In his view, teaching children could not be separated from the elements of human behavior that encouraged development of good persons. His graduate courses modeled the importance of teachers as good persons. Much of what he did validated teachers as persons and professionals. He discussed the need for teachers to write positive notes to pupils, parents, and teacher colleagues. He listened to teachers express frustrations and anger when they were not treated with respect by parents and supervisors. He worked to instill positive ways for his students to respond to difficult situations. Many of the projects his students developed addressed personal/psychological needs they'd experienced in their schools. In many respects, Richard's courses provided a safe place for teachers to work on issues within their schools and school systems.

There is no doubt that Richard walked to a different drummer (Peck 1987) and was successful in reaching teachers with his beliefs and vision. His courses consistently filled each semester, whereas the same was not true of professional colleagues. In the mid-nineties, Richard became the focus of complaints by other professors who contacted the university and stated that his courses lacked substance, were soft, and didn't require any serious study. To be more blatant, their concern was that teachers enrolled in his courses did so merely to acquire graduate hours. Inquiries by the university followed with a rather quick response from teachers who supported Richard. Dozens of letters from current and former teachers, administrators, and parents were sent to the president of the university and the head of the extension division, and they presented a different picture of his courses. A few examples highlight the views expressed in letters:

"Dr. Overfelt's unique teaching style is extremely helpful to veteran teachers who are looking for a model for themselves in these difficult times for teachers. He brings so many practical ideas that can be translated into making us better, more positive, and more productive teachers."

"Through classroom sharing with other teachers, I learned that I was not the only one who was experiencing the difficulties and demands that have recently surfaced with the ever-changing face of public education in the nineties."

"One of the course requirements that I have especially appreciated is a positive action plan for self-improvement. I believe this is an effective way to cause postgraduate students to reflect on their own effectiveness and to define their professional goals."

"Richard's classes, with their emphasis on the positive, help students to address important aspects of teaching and human relations: being a positive role model, communicating effectively with parents, giving sincere praise. Richard offers ample concrete, realistic examples on how to achieve these objectives."

"During this session, we worked on group presentations in MegaSkills, invitational education, school climate, and learning modalities. Dr. Overfelt is an excellent model of all the concepts he teaches. Through his courses, I am always rejuvenated and ready to go back to my classroom to implement new ideas."

There were no further complaints from colleagues, and Richard continued to follow his vision for effective teaching, based on sound human relations. His classes continued to attract large numbers of teachers.

Several experienced teachers were motivated to write books and pamphlets extolling the Overfelt vision of teaching and learning. These renderings recognized his knowledge and skill and came at a time when he was being criticized. The multitude of letters sent on his behalf by experienced teachers represented another form of recognition. The books and essays that teachers prepared highlighted aspects of his teaching that resonated with teachers. Two examples of teacher-produced writings are discussed below:

Richard's humanistic orientation led to a long list of pronouncements that came to be known as *The Sayings of Richard* (Eden 2016). They often appeared in discussions with pupils, teachers, and parents and were highly visible as printed placards on office walls, classrooms, and bulletin boards around school. In a few words, the sayings were a brief way of emphasizing the basic elements for the treatment of people. They were formalized as a booklet produced by one of his graduate students, titled *The Sayings of Richard: Wisdom on the Craft of Teaching and Being a Better Person*. The booklet of twenty-four pages contained twenty of Richard's sayings and included quotations and artistic renderings. A few representative examples are included here:

"Raise the praise, minimize the criticize." Focus on what a student does well.

"There are no gifted children; all children have gifts." Treat every student with respect and set them up for success.

"Make positive phone calls and write happy notes as much as possible." Show you are genuinely interested in a student's success and well-being.

"It's all about the kids." The single most important thing about successful education is the personal relationship between student and teacher. Students who feel that their teachers are invested in them and their success stand a better chance to learn.

"Respect, responsibility, and accountability." Be where you're supposed to be, when you're supposed to be there, with the stuff you're supposed to have, whether you want to or not.

"When it comes to learning, kids have their own clock." Be patient. Be understanding. Be supportive. And the student will be successful.

Another teacher wrote a dedication to Richard and his daughter, Ricci, also a teacher, who often assisted him with his classes. The book recalled a different set of themes typical of the working relationships Richard had with his students. The book was titled *Happy Days* and began with a realistic view of perfection:

> A good teacher reaches 85 percent of the students 85 percent of the time. No one is perfect! Do not dwell on the 15/15. That can become your rabbit and you miss the elephant. The rabbits are the small things in teaching that may not really impact your day unless you let them. The elephant is the important things for your students that you and your students really need to focus on. Be the 85/85 teacher you can be, and you and your students will meet your goals and have success (Fink 2015).

Being a good person was synonymous with Highcroft Ridge School. It was a dominant theme expressed by Richard from the very beginning of school planning in January 1978. A description of a good person was included in a short paragraph in the *Happy Days* book:

> A 90/90 person is a good person. He or she does their best 90 percent of the time in 90 percent of life's situations. Again, no one is perfect. We all make mistakes. You are a good person.

In the life of a busy teacher, overt discussion of the humanity of personhood is seldom heard. By thinking and acting on human qualities, teachers felt understood, supported in the positive atmosphere of Richard's courses. Within this milieu, teachers created novel interventions for their classrooms.

Richard's longevity in higher education provided a mechanism for teachers to discover and rediscover their personal strengths. Richard was well known in the metropolitan area and state for his support of the professional development of teachers. In August 2017, the *St. Louis Post-Dispatch* featured a front-page article about Richard and his work with teachers. The article displayed a series of pictures of Richard working with teachers on activities, including a teacher receiving an award on the rose rug. National recognition of his efforts came later that year, when Richard was the subject of an NBC program led by Rehema Ellis and airing nationwide. He who worked his entire life to recognize children and teachers was recognized for his dedication and service to children and teachers.

Final Thoughts

Richard's professional career as teacher, curriculum director, assistant superintendent, elementary school principal, and adjunct professor of education spanned seventy-four years. Such a wide-ranging career may not have been predicted for a rowdy boy who grew up in rural Northeast Missouri. However, the potential for achieving significant things was influenced by parents who knew what was necessary for being successful in life. The Great Depression taught everyone the importance of work—the key to survival during that period. The climb to higher order thinking and planning was a struggle for Richard and revealed a tenacity and determination that eventually carried him a great distance.

His experiences in Duncans Bridge shaped a set of beliefs and values that were tightly woven in his character. The ability to take risks, ask for help when needed, have sensitivity to others, and show empathy were formed early in life, and this directly related to his ability to include people in activities he led. Although he probably wasn't aware of the complexities of educational change that I have attempted to describe here, his natural gravitation to people made him an ideal leader for a self-organizing system of change.

Ralph Waldo Emerson (1992) wrote an essay on self-reliance in 1841, and a quote from his writing serves as a summary of Richard's life as a school leader. Emerson said, "An institution is the lengthened shadow of one man. His character determines the character of the organization." Some readers might question this reference to Richard's life as a leader. Richard himself would probably question it because successful institutions involve the contributions of many. However, in most successful organizations, there can be found a person or a small group who has an idea they seek to promote and develop. There is often one prime mover, provocateur, or wise and experienced person who begins a process that ultimately becomes a new endeavor. Richard was clearly a man who understood that any worthwhile project that seeks to make an impact on the world requires the investment of energy from many. Having said this, however, I return to Emerson's thesis that self-reliance is the granular material for success in leading one's life or leading an organization.

Richard came from modest origins and was humbled by the

adversity that his family and friends endured during the Depression. That period cut deep into his psyche and in large measure influenced his character development. Hardship can be a great teacher if one has support from parents and people in a small close-knit rural community like Duncans Bridge. The seeds of leadership were nurtured in that environment, where interdependence was a common thread. The mixture of genetics shaped by his environment influenced latent leadership potential—kindness, honesty, determination, concern for people experiencing difficulty, the capacity for listening and caring—and drew people into his sphere of influence. These elements of awakened leadership were enhanced by years of practice as a teacher and school administrator. Richard invested himself in the service of others, who admired and appreciated him as an example of a good person who cast a long shadow of success, often in the face of difficult circumstances.

His personal and professional life is replete with examples of how he exercised his service to others. I witnessed firsthand how he related to people in Duncans Bridge who knew him growing up. During a visit I made there in 1999, people spoke lovingly about Richard, his sense of humor and willingness to help others. Richard and his wife, Myra, responded to people in need by providing food and financial assistance. During his tenure as a principal, it was common for both of them to respond with food for teachers or members of their family who were ill or hospitalized. Richard often reached out to teachers and others who experienced life-changing circumstances. He was not a regular churchgoing man, but his humanity revealed deep beliefs that could only be explained by a religious outlook.

Richard and Myra had three children who attended white middle class schools. Richard wanted his children to understand that schools varied considerably in terms of diversity and degree of wealth. He addressed this concern by taking the children back to Duncans Bridge at regular intervals to expand their awareness of life in less fortunate circumstances. The children worked on the small farm that he and Myra owned near Duncans Bridge. They became acquainted with the local people and observed their father engaging in positive interactions with those he knew. All three children were college educated and were very successful in their professions. The children have continued Richard and Myra's legacy of sensitivity to people who are in need.

However, there was another dimension to Richard's leadership style that some would say was atypical but obvious when beliefs and values were at stake. Earlier in the narrative, I stated teachers and staff described him as "demanding and giving"; I recall a Highcroft parent volunteer describing him in a similar manner. Richard was determined to succeed, something he learned early in Duncans Bridge. He was not immune to bouts of depression, especially when his schedule became difficult to manage. When it came to the schooling of children, he was tenacious in expecting teachers and staff to treat children with respect and to be patient, caring, and compassionate. He was rarely impulsive, but when it came to what was best for his schoolchildren, he was straightforward and occasionally profane in speaking his truth to those who occupied positions of power and authority. Thus he was admired by most, disliked by a few, but loved by teachers who understood he was working to serve their best interests in teaching children.

As I wrap up this story, I remember a recent gathering of teachers that Richard orchestrated. Those attending were largely charter members of the original Highcroft staff from 1978. The meeting was full of good humor as the participants reflected on the challenges and successes of those early years. After it was over, Richard prepared and sent everyone a summary of the important things they had accomplished: the beliefs and values they had attached to building good persons. His comments represented everyone in the group. He concluded with the following:

Please find below some of the thoughts we shared in our closing circle:

We are good persons—85/85 and 90/90. We love life. I did the best I could with whatever came my way. I model "good stuff" for the persons in my school life. I don't ever remember thinking as I got ready for school, *I am going to school today to see if I can screw up a kid or two.* I'm proud of all I did to make Highcroft Ridge Elementary School so special and a great place to grow. Most of the time it was done my way because I did understand ...

If the heart is empty, it doesn't make any difference how full the head.

From the beginning, we built relationships. Somehow we understood the importance of relationships before business.

The relationships still stand the evidence. Here we are together.

REFERENCES

Bandura, A. 1997. *Self-Efficacy: The Exercise of Control.* New York: W. H. Freeman and Company.

Barth, R. 1986. "On Sheep and Goats and School Reform." *Phi Delta Kappan.* 68,(4) 293–96.

Barth, R. 1991. "Restructuring Schools: Some Questions for Teachers and Principals." *Phi Delta Kappan.* 73 (2) 123–28.

Beabout, B. R. 2012. "Turbulence, Perturbance, and Educational Change." *Complicity: An International Journal of Complexity and Education.* 2 (9) 15–29.

Byrk, A., P. Sebring, D. Kerbow, S. Rollow, and J. Easton. 1998. *Charting Chicago School Reform.* Boulder, CO: Westview Press.

Chen, G., and P. D. Bliese. 2002. "The Role of Different Levels of Leadership in Predicting Self and Collective Efficacy: Evidence for Discontinuity." *Journal of Applied Psychology* 87, no. 3: 549–56.

Collins, J. 2001. *Good to Great: Why Some Companies Make the Leap ... and Others Don't.* New York: HarperCollins.

Denzin, N. 1970. *The Research Act: A Theoretical Introduction to Sociological Methods.* Chicago: Aldine.

Dewey, J., 1916. *Democracy and Education.* New York: Free Press.

Dewey, J., 1997 *Experience and Education*. New York: Touchstone Publications.

Dozier, B. 2014. *Leaders Are Born, Not Made*. Wordpress.com weblog, July 23, 2014.

Dufour, R. 2004. "What Is a Professional Learning Community?" *Educational Leadership*, 61(8), 6–11.

Eden, M., Seibe, T. and Marks, S. 2016. *The Sayings of Richard*. Unpublished book.

Emerson, R. W. 1992. *The Selected Writings of Ralph Waldo Emerson*. The Modern Library Edition. New York: Random House.

Fink, J. 2015. *Happy Days*. Unpublished book.

Firestone, R., Firestone, L., and Catlett. 2013. *The Self under Siege: A Therapeutic Model for Differentiation*. Routledge: CRC Press.

Fullan, M. 2002. "Principals as Leaders in a Culture of Change." *Educational Leadership*.

Fullan, M. 1972. "Overview of the Innovative Process and the User." *Interchange. 3, 1–46*.

Fullan, M. 2006. *Turnaround Leadership*. San Francisco: Josey-Bass.

George, P. 1975. "Ten Years of Open Space Schools; a Review of the Research." *Florida Research and Development Council*, Gainesville: University of Florida Press.

Glaser, B. G., and Strauss, A. L. 1967. *The Discovery of Grounded Theory: Strategies for Qualitative Research*. Chicago: Aldine.

Godwin, D. K., *Leadership in Turbulent Times*. New York, NY: Simon & Schuster.

Gronn, P. 2008. "The Future of Distributed Leadership." *Journal of Educational Administration*. 46 (2), 604–605.

Hargreaves, A. and Fink, D., 2006. *Sustainable Leadership*. San Francisco: Jossey-Bass.

Harris, A., 2009. *Distributive Leadership: Different Perspective*. (Ed.), London: Springer.

Heifetz, R. 1994. *Leadership without Easy Answers*. Cambridge, MA: Harvard University Press.

House, R., Rousseau, D., and Thomas-Hunt, M. 1995. "The Meso Paradigm: A Framework for the Integration of Micro and Macro Organizational Behavior." *Research in Organizational Behavior*, 17, 71–115, 967.

Jappinen, A. K. 2014. "The Emergence of Human Interactional Sense Making Process as a Complex System." *Complicity: An International Journal of Complexity and Education*. 11 (2). 65–85.

Klein, H., Sayama, M., Faratin, P. and Bar-Yam, Y. 2003. "The Dynamics of Collaborative Design: Insights from Complex Systems and Negotiation Research." *Concurrent Engineering*. 11 (3) 201-209.

Lewin, K. 1951. *Field Theory and Social Science*. New York: Harpers.

Lichtenstein, B.B. and Plowman, D. 2009. "The Leadership of Emergence: A Complex Systems Leadership Theory of Emergence at Successive Organizational Levels." *The Leadership Quarterly*. 20 (4) 617–630.

MacBeath, J. 2005. "Leadership as Distributed: A Matter of Practice." *School Leadership and Management.* 25 (4) 349–366.

Maslow, A. 1998 *Maslow on Management.* New York, NY: John Wiley & Sons.

Maslow, A. 1965. "Observing and Reporting Education Experiments." *Humanist.* 25 (13).

Marques, J. 2010. "Awakened Leaders: Born or Made?" *Leadership & Organization Development Journal. 31 (4).*

Miles, M. B. 1964. "On Temporary Systems." In M. B. Miles (Ed) *Innovations in Education.* New York NY, Teachers College Press.

Mosher, G. W., 1981. *Individualized & Systemic Changes Mediated by a Small Educational Grant Program.* Teachers' Center Exchange Program of Research on Experienced Teacher Centers. San Francisco, CA: Far West Laboratory for Educational Research & Development.

Overfelt, R. 1978. *Planning for a New School.* Unpublished paper.

Pascale, R. T., Millemann, M., and Giola, L. 2000. *Surfing the Edge of Chaos.* New York: Three Rivers Press.

Peck, S. M. 1987. *The Different Drum: Steps in Community Making and Peace.* New York: Simon & Schuster.

Ravitch, D. 1983. *The Troubled Crusade.* New York: Basic Books.

Plowman, D. A., Silansky, Kulkarni, M and Travis. 2007. "The Role of Leadership in Emergent, Self-Organization." *The Leadership Quarterly.* 18, 341–356.

Sarason, S. 1982. *The Culture of the School and the Problem of Change.* Boston: Allyn & Bacon.

Senge, P. 1990. *The Fifth Discipline: The Art and Practice of the Learning Organization.* New York: Doubleday.

Smith, S., and Scott, J. 1990. "The Collaborative School: A Work Environment for Effective Instruction". *National Association of Secondary School Principals.* Reston, VA.

Smith, L.M. and Keith, P. 1971. *Anatomy of Educational Innovation: Analysis of an Elementary School.* New York, NY: Wiley.

Wagner, T. 2001. "Leadership for Learning: An Action Theory of School Change." *Phi Delta Kappan.* 82 (5) 378-83.

Waldman, A., Barnard, M. and Walter. 2009. "Leadership and Outcomes of Performance Appraisal Process." *Journal of Occupational Psychology.* 60(3) 177–186.

Weick, K.E., Sutcliffe, K.M. and Obstfed, D. 2005 "Organizing and Process of Sense Making." *Organization Science.* 16 (4), 409–421.